BLACK COOKSTOVE

BLACK

COOKSTOVE

MEDITATIONS ON LITERATURE, CULTURE,
AND CUISINE IN COLOMBIA

· · · · · · · ·

GERMÁN PATIÑO OSSA
Translated by Jonathan Tittler

THE PENNSYLVANIA STATE UNIVERSITY PRESS
UNIVERSITY PARK, PENNSYLVANIA

Library of Congress Cataloging-in-Publication Data

Names: Patiño Ossa, Germán, author. | Tittler, Jonathan,
    1945– translator.
Title: Black cookstove : meditations on literature,
    culture, and cuisine in Colombia / Germán Patiño
    Ossa ; translated by Jonathan Tittler.
Other titles: Fogón de negros. English
Description: University Park, Pennsylvania : The
    Pennsylvania State University Press, [2020] |
    Translation of Fogón de negros: cocina y cultura
    en una región latinoamericana. | Includes
    bibliographical references and index.
Summary: "Examines the hybrid cuisine of the Cauca
    Valley in Colombia, exploring cooking in literature
    and practice as a symbolic representation of social
    relations and a system of social communication, with
    particular attention to the role of Afro-descendant
    women"—Provided by publisher.
Identifiers: LCCN 2020035731 | ISBN 9780271086989
    (paperback)
Subjects: LCSH: Isaacs, Jorge, 1837–1895. María. |
    Food habits—Colombia—Cauca River Valley.
    | Cooking—Social aspects—Colombia—Cauca
    River Valley. | Cooking in literature. | Cauca River
    Valley (Colombia)—History. | Cauca River Valley
    (Colombia)—Social conditions. | Cauca River Valley
    (Colombia)—Race relations—History.
Classification: LCC GT2853.C7 P3813 2011 | DDC
    394.1/20986153—dc23
LC record available at https://lccn.loc.gov/2020035731

The Pennsylvania State University Press is a member of
the Association of University Presses.

It is the policy of The Pennsylvania State University
Press to use acid-free paper. Publications on uncoated
stock satisfy the minimum requirements of American
National Standard for Information Sciences—
Permanence of Paper for Printed Library Material, ANSI
z39.48-1992.

CONTENTS

· ·

ILLUSTRATIONS

....

TRANSLATOR'S FOREWORD

My deepest gratitude goes to the following people and institutions, for their invaluable support in helping ensure that this book could reach completion: Germán Patiño Ossa, whose understated brilliance I hope shines palpably throughout this text, despite numerous losses and occasional gains produced by the translation process; Isabel Patiño Collazos, Germán's daughter, who, upon the author's untimely death, valiantly persisted in securing the documentation necessary for the production of this book; to my former colleague María Antonia Garcés, whose knowledge of, passion for, and commitment to Cauca Valley cooking and culture are without equal; Tim Keppel, for his stylistic acuity in both Spanish and English, his companionship, and his guidance through the Cali Zoo; Darío Henao Restrepo, colleague and friend, for facilitating key relationships early in this process; Luisa Ungar, for her sound advice on graphic design; José Antonio Carbonell Blanco and Camila Cesarino Costa, for permission to reproduce many of the images that illustrate this text; the Convenio Andrés Bello, for streamlining the transfer of translation rights; Ellie Goodman, executive editor of Penn State University Press, for her sharp critical eye and collaborative editorial style; and my wife, Susan, for her profound understanding of cuisine and nourishment, and the difference between the two.

JONATHAN TITTLER

PRESENTATION

....

The Andrés Bello Prize for Iberian American thought, as stipulated in its tenets, is intended to exalt and stimulate the work of intellectuals in the region, on topics that tend to foster the integration of our peoples and to highlight their characteristic cultural diversity. It is proposed that the presented works convey values that help build a decent world and a region of greater social justice. It purports, in addition, that to attain this end one must emphasize, as has been declared by the ministers of education of the signatory nations, the inalienable right to education that in many of these nations is a constitutional mandate.

The present publication, awarded first prize in the category of essay by the international jury consisting of the Ecuadorian historian Enrique Ayala Mora, the Colombian writer Roberto Rubiano Vargas, and the Peruvian poet Mirko Lauer, constitutes a study—documented and poetically composed, on a region in the southwest of Colombia—that may well serve as a model for approaches to any region of Latin America. The author conveys to us, through a process of recovery of suggestive historical sources and of meticulous personal inquiry, how gastronomy and the "culinary arts" of a given geographic zone, in which over time diverse ethnic groups have merged together—with special regard to the descendants of African slaves—reveal a dense network of significant relations. There one sees reflected the life and tensions of the community, with its elaborate cultural expressions, among which are the refined and imaginative devices that make eating a function that is not only physiological but also highly symbolic and sensorial.

We hope, with the activity generated by the Andrés Bello Prize, to support and substantively endow a shared space of qualified information, centered on the reflection and interpretation of our realities, cultural expressions, and history, which permits the dissemination and free flow of knowledge and thought on the integration of our peoples.

FRANCISCO HUERTA MONTALVO—JUNE 2007
Executive Secretary
Andrés Bello Council
Santafé de Bogotá, Colombia

AUTHOR'S PREFACE

· ·

[Translator's note: In January 2015, when this book, whose origins date back to 2009, was nearing completion, word arrived of the author Germán Patiño Ossa's untimely death. Although the book manuscript was all but complete, certain bibliographic details, especially the page references of numerous quotations, were not yet obtained and therefore remain unknown. Fortunately, by the time of German's death, this preface was already written and could be translated. Only minor stylistic changes have been introduced since then.]

The editors of the US edition of *Black Cookstove* have invited me to write some words of introduction, with the goal of making the text more readily understandable to English-speaking readers—a necessary but difficult task to accomplish, in my case. Though I have some North American ancestry—my great-grandfather was William Barney Crane, a southerner who came to live in Colombia's Cauca River Valley—what I know about the United States is not so much from real-life experience as it is a product of multiple readings and the influence of US culture through the mass media, especially the movies.

I have visited the States, perfunctorily, wandering through the streets of New York, Baltimore, Miami, New Orleans, and Las Vegas, always on work assignments and for brief stays. I remember a tongue-and-pastrami sandwich with mustard, unforgettable for its flavor and Rabelaisian immensity, in Manhattan; likewise a delicious gumbo, with its unique flavor and texture of okra, along the banks of the Mississippi; and a demitasse of sweet black Cuban coffee, in Miami. I have felt the attractive vitality and dynamism there, but I have only the slightest hint of what US Americans think or feel. How, then, to help someone understand the cultural universe of Colombia, and in particular its Cauca Valley region, which is the space in which *Black Cookstove* takes place? I am happy to make the attempt, as best as I can; besides, I find appealing the opportunity to respond to a few critical readings of my book that have emerged from among Colombian academics.

Before anything else I must say that I am fortunate to have had Jonathan Tittler as my translator. He is a distinguished North American scholar and an expert on Colombia, where he is highly regarded. His translation of the novel *Changó, the Biggest Badass*, by Manuel Zapata Olivella, makes a major contribution toward enabling a North American comprehension of Afro-Colombian culture and, through this comprehension, revealing the hidden black face of our national identity. Engraved in my memory are his courtesy, his uncomplicated manner, and his joy in sharing a cup of Colombian coffee in the front garden of a little hotel near the banks of the Cali River, focused on discussing a few terms from the book that are difficult to understand, even for Colombian readers. Also, I recall his amusement at finding himself in Cali's bullfight arena, amid the hypnotic sounds of the marimba, during an evening of competition in the captivating Petronio Alvarez Pacific Coast Music Festival. And his enthusiasm shone for our visit to chef Michael Lynch, a mix of a half-crazy US American with a crazy half Colombian, at his restaurant in Cali's historic San Antonio district, where he prepared for us a dish from *Black Cookstove*—creamy rice soup with pork—and delighted us with freshly brewed coffee, whose beans were roasted and ground on the premises.

I learned later that Tittler went with Tim Keppel, another US American but a resident of Cali, a professor of literature at the Universidad del Valle and one of today's best Colombian writers—I say Colombian because his work is both written and thought in Colombian Spanish—to visit the Cali zoo and see one of the animals that serves as hunting prey for a dish in *Black Cookstove*. That is an example of how punctilious and conscientious Jonathan is, which tells us a lot about the way he deals with the task of translating texts from a language that is not his own. He is a true maestro, for those who would dedicate themselves to this noble profession.

At this point I think it is time to let Kathleen Romoli speak. This North American historian lived and worked in Colombia and wrote a series of key texts on the ethnohistory of my country. She also felt the necessity to introduce Colombia to North American readers, and she wrote a highly valuable book in that regard, *Colombia, Gateway to South America*, published back in 1941. Despite the changes, at times dramatic, of the past seventy-five years, the country continues to be essentially the same one that Romoli encountered then.

To be sure, I invite my readers to consult that text, but I can't help but quote a fragment from Romoli here, even if just to give an idea of the quality of her prose and of her perspicacity:

> Colombia is, then, a land of extremes and contradictions. There are towering mountains marching in tremendous columns three abreast, some of them lifting snow-covered crests 18,000 feet in the air; there are simmering jungles, swampy and fever haunted, where crocodiles slide into the shallow water and parrots scream from trees grotesque with orchids. . . . Canoes carved from a single log paddle past the big steamers at the new Maritime Terminal; people on diminutive burros, riding high on the loads with their feet crossed like scissors on the animal's necks, skirt the aviation fields, jogging along asphalt highways to market.

There were colleges in Bogotá and Popayán when Williamsburg was undreamed of. . . . There are archeological mysteries, impassive and secretive, that research has not penetrated, treasures in gold and emeralds still undiscovered. There are Indians of all kinds, from the proud Putumayans to the shy tribes who burn their villages and move back into the jungle when the canoes of the outlanders become too frequent. Savants and medicine men, statesmen and aborigines, cocktails and *chicha* [corn beer], golf clubs and poisoned arrows, swimming pools and sacred lakes, Paris frocks, *ruanas* [heavy shawls] and breechclouts—they are all, in varying degrees, Colombia.[1]

If to the foregoing we add that Colombia contains some of the greatest biodiversity in the world, with its corresponding cultural diversity, we find ourselves in a true dilemma. The Native American substratum of Colombian culture also entails significant biodiversity. Colombia's current national territory was not part of a hegemonic empire, as occurred in Mexico and Peru, and therefore the Spanish conquistadors did not encounter a unified linguistic or political entity but rather multiple and differentiated communities, many of which were in mutual confrontation for control of their vital spaces. In each environmental niche of this land of intricate geography, there was a confluence of Spaniards from diverse places of origin who, in turn, came in contact with aborigines who belonged to different groups: people from Andalusia, the Canary Islands, Galicia, Extremadura, the Basque Country, Castile, and León connected with Chimilas, Zenúes, Chibchas, Pijaos, Wayús, Sindaguas, Andaquíes, Gorrones, Emberáes, and many more who, just like the conquistadors, had their own languages and cultures. In each region and each locale of the territory, therefore, the base of racial mixing produced highly differentiated communities. Add to this the subsequent arrival of African slaves, also of diverse ancestry: Yoruba, Bantu, Congo, Fons, Carabalí, and so on, and you have an approximate picture of the diversity of racially mixed cultures, both regional and local, just as you have an explanation of why it was so hard for Colombia to consolidate as a unitary nation. So there is no one Colombia but various Colombias, and there is no one kind of Colombian but various Colombians. Romoli says something in this regard: "Heaven knows it is hard enough to say, in the time the social law allows, what an Englishman is like, or a Swede, or an Italian, unless blessed with the happy certainty of the uninformed. But it is child's play compared to describing a Colombian, if by that is meant a citizen of the Republic of Colombia. . . . In the widest sense of the word, a Colombian may be one of several extremes. He may be tall and blond and blue eyed, or small and brown and Asiatic looking. Or he may be black."[2]

He or she is still that way today, which explains why *Black Cookstove* concentrates on several of those various Colombias and their corresponding types of

Colombians, even though in the particular regions one finds the same diversity of citizens that Romoli mentions. The geographic section of Colombia about which I write is often confused with the Departamento del Valle [Cauca Valley State], an administrative division of the Republic of Colombia situated in the southwest of the country. It lies partially between two great mountain ranges (the Western and the Central Andes), has an extreme western boundary on the Pacific coast, and is named for the great inter-Andean valley formed by the Cauca River. Kathleen Romoli lived and grounded much of her work there, and she described it in the following manner:

> In Colombia when one says "the Valley" it means the valley of the Cauca, the lovely, fertile strip between the coastal ranges and the central Cordillera where it is always June. A hundred and fifty miles long by fifteen or twenty broad, it lies at 3,000 feet or more above sea level, a little Eden guarded by the Andes. Its beauty has not the intemperance of the *selva* [jungle] or the bleak magnificence of the high plateaus: this is the Happy Valley, peaceful, fecund and comforting.
>
> Until the turn of the century, this was a largely cattle land, given over to *latifundia* [large landholdings] where life was patriarchal and unchanging. Cali was a rural center of perhaps fifteen thousand people; the Department of Cauca still included the greater part of the old *gobernación* [provincial government] of Belalcázar, with Popayán as its capital. Traveling was by horse or mule; three or four days to Popayán, ten to Pasto and ten or fifteen to Bogotá. Agitation for a railway was already strong, but many people agreed with that *hacendado* [landholder] who refused to allow a right-of-way across his land.

With this established I believe a summary of the history of this territory is in order.

At least ten thousand years ago, groups of humans populated territory of the regions known today as the Cauca Valley. Situated at first at the headwaters of the Calima River, they covered the territory of the inter-Andean valley formed there, and later they dispersed toward various areas, reaching as far as the Pacific coast, the mountainous north, and the level plain of the geographic valley of the Cauca River. They ruled for thousands of years, developed an agrarian lifestyle in harmony with the natural environment, had their own religious cults, created stable settlements that held the land communally, and, in some periods, achieved elevated artistry in works of ceramics and gold metallurgy.

They were displaced, or conquered, by Amerindians from other lands, who set up chiefdoms, spread throughout the entire territory, which were interconnected by a multitude of roads, along which they traded and which, by the same token, facilitated confrontations, tribal wars, and even plundering. Conflict between the communities was not, however, the principal aspect of their way of life, but rather exchange, commerce, and an awareness that the earth, mother of all goods, belonged to all.

In the year 1535 of our era, that long and slow history came to an end. A collective drama descended on the settlers of the Cauca River Valley: warriors armed with technologies that had never been seen before, accompanied by black slaves who were tall and extraordinarily strong, and dogs of war even more ferocious than their masters, initiated a new conquest of the territory, without showing or asking for mercy. They were Spaniards and Africans from very far away, and for them the land belonged not to all but to those who appropriated it. They even appropriated other human beings. Tempered during eight long centuries of domination and conflict with the Arabs, they were experts in prolonged battles, and they were moved by a religion—Catholicism—that ordered them to conquer the world for their God.

They furthermore had the help of new diseases that decimated the Americans. Even so the ancestral occupants of the Cauca River Valley fought with such ferocity and valor that it took the Spaniards almost a century to pacify the territory and establish the settlements they founded. In the end almost nothing remained of the original occupants of the land, who either were annihilated or fled toward impenetrable jungles. The few who remained have languished since then in positions of subalternity.

For four centuries, from the beginning of the sixteenth century through the first half of the twentieth, the descendants of Spaniards, Africans, and Native Americans coexisted in the Cauca River Valley, organizing the territory in the manner of medieval Spain, basing human relations on the private possession of material goods. There emerged a new society, stratified and hybrid, united in language and religion, which would engender a new culture that was not Spanish or African or Native American. It was Creole and was peculiar to the Cauca River Valley. It was also a rich society, as abundant gold deposits were discovered in the region of Caloto, near Cartago, and in countless rivers that flow into the Pacific Ocean. A regime of livestock ranches and sugarcane plantations, combined with the mining operations, characterized Cauca Valley society. A million head of cattle grazed in the Cauca River Valley at the start of the nineteenth century. But this society was subject to a distant monarchy, to which it was less and less obedient.

The consolidation of Cauca Valley culture, with its peculiar way of speaking, its growing mulatto population, its particular tendencies, its own traditions and customs, its crafts suited to the climate of the tropics, and the development of a tradition of literacy strengthened feelings of autonomy that took political form in 1810—as happened in the rest of Spanish America—when the reign of Ferdinand VII was toppled by Napoleon's forces, with the king himself taken prisoner.

But the Creole elite were distant from the common people and wanted to be treated like Spaniards even though they no longer were Spanish. Because of this paradox, although they achieved autonomy for a brief period by not aspiring to independence and the construction of a new nation, they facilitated a Spanish Reconquest, and the region found itself sunken again in a long and fierce struggle. In the end, as part of a new sovereign state now known as Colombia, the Cauca Valley has navigated through a period of republican life pregnant with contradictions and disputes, while the process of transculturation begun in 1535 continues unabated. In spite of political independence, slavery remained in effect in Colombia until the second half of the nineteenth century. And its stigmas still impact Cauca Valley society, as does the survival of the colonial way of life, with its great social inequalities, the disparity in the distribution of incomes, and the network of social loyalties that tends to favor a small circle of the economic elite.

Despite all these continuities, the region has changed substantially over the past two centuries. It was transformed from a bucolic region, where the population was stagnant or on occasion diminished, to an industrialized territory, densely populated and crisscrossed by modern roads, featuring a commercial life that is active and increasingly democratic. The link to the Pacific with the construction of the port of Buenaventura, along with the completion of the railroad, which coincided with the opening of the Panama Canal, produced a substantial upheaval: it changed the axis of the coffee trade, Colombia's main export product until the 1970s, displacing it from the Atlantic coast to the Pacific and transforming the Cauca Valley into an essential region for the national economy. Later the industrialization of the sugarcane plantations would change forever the territory's rural life, opening the way to the urban lifestyle that predominates today.

All these dramatic changes, begun in 1535, have modeled the Cauca Valley State we know today, an administrative entity that barely encompasses part of the Cauca Valley region from a historical and cultural perspective. Migratory waves of Lithuanians, Japanese, Germans, North Americans, Italians, French, Syrian-Lebanese, and Portuguese, to which are added peoples from Ecuador and the Colombian regions of Antioquia, Huila, Nariño, Tolima, and Cundinamarca, among others, have also contributed to create a cosmopolitan region, open to all manner of influences, where one can breathe the beneficial air of universality. As happens when we peel away the layers of an onion, however, in the heart of the region we find the descendants of Spaniards and Africans, over a bed of Native Americans, lending to the Cauca Valley its uniqueness and spiritual depth. These descendants are the soul of our history and the blood of our cultural anatomy.

One of the decisive factors in the development of this region resides in the strong opposition of the native communities to Spanish domination—and its analogue, the extinction of a major part of the original native peoples. So it was that, at the end of the conquest, in the late sixteenth century, the Spaniards found themselves without a labor force with which to exploit the estates and mines. They needed to acquire, and in growing quantities, African slaves, who thrived in the prolific Cauca Valley habitat. Known censuses from the end of the colonial period (traditionally set at 1810) show that people of color (black, mulatto, or any shade that indicated hybridizing with even a drop of African blood) constituted a majority of the region's population. Thus, the process of racial mixing consisted, above all, of a process of *mulataje* (Africanizing).

In this region you cannot avoid the presence of what we might call *Afro-descendants*, both in the physical type of its inhabitants and in the hidden corners of their spirituality. Really, the same goes for the entire nation as well, for Colombia is the country with the greatest number of Afro-descendants in the Americas, after Brazil and the United States. Most of them are concentrated along the Caribbean and Pacific coasts, including in the latter the Cauca River Valley. Cali, the capital city of the state simply called "Valle," is, after Bahia, in Brazil, the city with the most Afro-descendants in Latin America.

Cauca Valley inhabitants, therefore, although they may be blond, fair-skinned, and blue-eyed, bear within them the imprint of blackness: in their speech, their gestures, and their taste for polyrhythmic music; their inclination toward a certain kind of cooking; their Catholicism imbued with pagan hymns; and, of course, their passion for partying and dancing. Isolated from the rest of the world, they have coexisted with blacks for five centuries, and they have learned—on many occasions from their black nanny—about everything in life. To be sure, the stigma of slavery whips them and they seem preternaturally impelled, especially when mingling among the upper classes, to suffer from an anachronistic racism, feeling themselves to be the lord of the black element that surrounds them. But they cannot escape from that atmosphere of negritude, which grows ever larger and more vigorous. That has been my own experience, and, in some sense, is what has led me to write this book.

When I hear the word *cooking*—not *gastronomy* or *menu* or *recipe* but *cooking*, or perhaps even *kitchen*—two women come to my mind: Lourdes and Jesusita. They take me directly back to my infancy, but always with the idea that *cooking* is the correct term by which to designate those life-giving, delectable, and at times even voluptuous preparations they raised me to expect. But in common parlance *kitchen* refers to the site, to the space where these women and others like them worked, amid an endless prattle that dealt with matters of life or death— "So-and-so is pregnant"; "Thus-and-so is involved with Joe Blow, the husband of thus-and-such"; "John Doe's nieces are carrying on with the twin thugs"; and other dramas of the sort—as they produced their steaming and aromatic dishes wrapped in leaves or their colorful rice or refreshing almond milk. The kitchen is really a female temple where priestesses of good taste and vital restoration officiate. I suppose it has always been that way, or it ought to have been.

I remember Lourdes, a young mulatto woman from Rio de Janeiro, with a contagious laugh and a tender heart. My parents' occupations, as students at the Federal University of Rio, did not allow them to spend much time with us—that is, my siblings and me. So we were under the care of Lourdes, who during the day would hum the sambas that were in style: "Si pensa que cachaza e agua, cachaza non e agua, nao" (If you think that rum is water, rum is not water, no), while she was busy preparing the meal. It still makes me smile to remember that when I came home from school, tired, dirty, and sweaty, it was Lourdes who greeted us with a glass of lemonade made with coconut water or a pitcher overflowing with golden pineapple juice. Lourdes was our joy of every single day. "Venhan meus meninos a jantar" (Come, my children, to eat), she would say in a singsong voice I will never forget, while she removed from the kitchen tin magnificent dishes of white rice, black beans, and *farofa*, that mixture of tapioca flour, butter, onions, scrambled eggs, and salt and pepper, which adorns with its flavor and texture all of Brazilian cooking and without which life would be incomplete.

Of course, Lourdes did not think that anyone else knew anything about cooking, particularly the Portuguese and in general the Europeans, whom she generically called *gringos*. "Portugués non sabe de jantar, nao" (The Portuguese don't know anything about eating, no), she would say, with her characteristic double negative. Nor did she believe in recipe books. I never saw a cookbook in Lourdes's pantry. She would actually have preferred to die than to be caught with a cookbook in her hands. For any self-respecting traditional Afro-American woman, to read a cookbook would suggest that she hadn't paid attention to her mother's lessons, that she did not know how to cook, that she did not know how to care for her man. Or worse, it meant that her mother was negligent and did not guide her as to a proper and adequate woman's role. And this extends to child rearing, sex, and funeral rites, which is to say, everything that is truly important in life.

Of course, her cooking knew nothing of grams, ounces, or exact measurements. A little of this, a smidgen of that, a dash of the other: mix, bake, and taste. Adjust if necessary and transmit what was learned in each cooking session from generation to generation, in such a way that a dish prepared today represents the accumulated wisdom of two hundred years. We are talking about a way of cooking where things are made with the hands, where flavors are transmitted almost genetically: touch and taste, but especially touch. It is a cooking of senses and sentiment, real magic and no science. "A ciencia non sabe de jantar, nao" (Science doesn't know about eating, no), she would say whimsically.

It was the same with Jesusita, a few years later, when we were no longer in Rio de Janeiro but in Cali. From the Pacific coastal city of Tumaco, she was also a young mulatto woman, although a little darker, but just as prone to a singsong. "Oye qué bonito lo vienen bajando, con ramos de flores lo están arrullando" (See how sweetly they are taking him down, with bouquets of flowers they lull him), she would sing with a lovely voice, and that tune has been etched in my memory ever since. We lived in Miraflores, across from the park, now without my mother, for which reason Jesusita was our full-time nanny.

Not counting the difference in their physical appearance, Lourdes and Jesusita were much the same. The Tumacan didn't believe in recipes either, and she kept up a constant dispute with my stepmother on all matters culinary. Of course, it always seemed to me that Jesusita really did know a lot about cooking and that my stepmother did not. Perhaps there was some sort of complicity between us. I don't know what this Afro-Tumacan woman saw in me. I don't know what she liked about this child who lived playing an eternal soccer match, who brought her nothing more than dirty shirts, muddy shoes, and torn trousers, but every time I was scolded by my parents, Jesusita would come to my defense by ceasing to speak to them. She, who was all laughter and jokes, treated them coolly, always serious and indifferent, until they apologized in some way (the best way was with a gift for me).

Perhaps because I shared a bedroom with Muchilanga, an ugly, skinny kid, quite a bit older than me—he must have been about eighteen—who sent Jesusita little letters, I found myself reading those letters aloud to her (she couldn't read), and I additionally passed her messages back to the odious Muchilanga, who took her out to the movies at least once on a Sunday morning. Through Muchilanga I learned that "hot" could refer to things other than the meals that Jesusita used to prepare. For example, Jesusita herself could be hot, an expression I did not understand until much later.

Much as Lourdes introduced me to the unforgettable flavor of *farofa*, Jesusita allowed me to come to know the festival that consists of rice with coconut. And I must confess that I learned to make it from my nanny and that with it on more than one occasion she got me out of a jam. I was invited to many parties at the university because I would bring, or I prepared, that dish. Graceful girls from the University of the Andes gave me—small, poor, and timid—the time of day because I would take Jesusita's dish to the party. By then I knew that those nymphs were "hot," truly as hot as Jesusita's rice with coconut. And that is no small thing.

But what Jesusita was about, just as what Lourdes was about, was cooking in the fullest sense of the word. It is something that you pick up from your grandmother, and you can learn only by the fire of the kitchen stove, something sensitive and alive that always tastes great. Glory for me consisted of returning home from a soccer match and, after being bawled out by Jesusita for the disaster of my torn clothing—her scoldings were always the same and were the only reproofs I accepted with pleasure—I was compensated with a dish of white rice and slices of fried ripe plantains, with a beautiful fried egg, the white solid and the yolk runny, crowning it all. It was then, and it is still now, despite the deformation of my palate from so much academic study, my favorite dish. *Black Cookstove* celebrates, in some way, that kind of cooking. That which comes to us from our Afro-descendant roots, intimately linked to Colombia's Pacific coast and, in the end, just as native to the Cauca River Valley as yucca bread, sweetened lemon compote, and cottage cheese with sugarcane syrup.

To be sure, there is something in what I am saying that goes far beyond recipe books and warm personal memories. Cooking is a process that encompasses the production and acquisition of ingredients; the transformation of prime materials; the distribution, preparation, consumption, and utilization of the discards—a complex series that, at each step, implies the establishment of social relations that constitute the key to culinary understanding. It is not so much a matter of ingredients or recipes as it is of relations between human beings. Cooking must be viewed as an essential element of culture, right alongside language, with which it shares many characteristics: it identifies, communicates, symbolizes, and groups communities that are sometimes vast and finds a common thread of their cultural personality in language and cooking. That is why I say the whole purpose of *Black Cookstove* is to explore the nature of cooking and kitchens and to give an account of the process of formation of a culture in a Colombian region of Latin America. It is a process that, despite its peculiarities, can serve as a matrix for similar studies in other regions and even for other thematic areas in the history of culture.

The crux of the matter resides in the concept of *transculturation*, which is crucial to a complete understanding of the text. Even though I use the term somewhat freely—not trying to specify the limits of its reach—I insist that I do so in the precise sense that the Cuban anthropologist Fernando Ortiz gives it in his *Contrapunteo cubano del tabaco y el azúcar* (Cuban counterpoint of tobacco and sugar): "The word *transculturation* best expresses the different phases of the transitive process from one culture to another, because this process does not consist of acquiring a different culture, which is what in all rigor is meant by the Anglo-American term *acculturation*, but rather it also necessarily implies the loss or uprooting of a previous culture, which could be called a partial *deculturation*, and, besides, it means the consequent creation of cultural phenomena that could be called *neoculturation*."[3] We are dealing with a phenomenon that resembles a chemical reaction, through which, by starting out with different cultures, a new culture is produced. In the process the original cultures lose some of their characteristics and acquire other new ones, as happens with the relation between hydrogen and oxygen when they form water.

Ortiz's concept received an enthusiastic statement of support from Bronislaw Malinowski, in the prologue to Ortiz's book. Malinowski eschewed the term *acculturation* because "it contains a whole combination of determined and inconvenient etymological implications. It is an ethnocentric term with a moral meaning. The immigrant has to 'acculturate,' as do the indigenous, pagans, infidels, barbarians, or savages who enjoy the 'benefit' of being subjected to our Great Western Culture." For the great Polish anthropologist, who resided in the United States, "any cultural change, or as we shall say from now on, any transculturation is a process in which one always gives something up in exchange for what one receives. . . . It is a process in which both sides of the equation come out modified . . . a process in which a new reality emerges . . . a new phenomenon, original and independent."[4]

This principle, the Cauca River Valley Creole identity resulting from a process of transculturation, runs throughout *Black Cookstove*. Although we can trace influences that are Spanish, Moorish, Bantu, and Inca, as well as those from other Native American communities, Cauca River Valley culture is a product different from all the others. Whether they are descendants of Spaniards, Africans, or Native Americans, they become Creoles, no matter their social condition, their racial configuration, or their specific belief system. They belong to the same culture, despite visible differences of fortune and power. To be sure, there are nuances to this scheme, but this basic outline still holds.

For my part I will say that the processes of transculturation suppose traumatic experiences, wars, dominations, and indignities. The natural tendency of cultures is to survive and maintain themselves in isolation from one another. A feeling of xenophobia (orig.: *héterofobia*) is characteristic of all human beings; we all fear, to one degree or another, that which strikes us as different or alien. It follows, then, that the formation of Cauca Valley culture stands against a background of violence, spoils, and slavery. This is analogous to the labor pains that precede any childbirth. Amid the barbarity and domination, the subjugated groups developed strategies of survival that provided them with the best existence possible, within the given limitations. Manacled and muzzled slaves knew that learning the language of the master would bring them certain advantages. Native Americans learned to appreciate the introduced domestic animals, when overhunting decimated their prey. And the same goes for the dominant groups: the Spanish, who so disdained and distrusted the Indian, had to learn to eat maize, along with other American products, if they wanted to survive in their deranged enterprise of conquest.

In this primitive world of exchanges, the bulk of which were imposed, the foundations of the new Creole culture were set. And Afro-descendants played a special role there, insofar as creativity in the kitchen was concerned. Their contribution was not the introduction of African ingredients, for the slave-trade system did not permit that much. All that mythology about pigeon pea or okra seeds hidden in the tight kink of their hair is no more than a nice way of praising the intelligence and astuteness of the black person, a show of empathy toward an oppressed population, but there is no surviving documentation for such ruses. The truth is that most customary foodstuffs in Africa were transported by the slavers themselves, with the less-than-noble motive of cheapening the slaves' diet, as occurred in the cases of plantain, rice, and yam.

Nonetheless, the role of Afro-descendants has proven to be essential. They were a type of bridge that served as the conveyor between the culinary knowledge of the Native Americans and that of the Iberians, providing the sauce that blended together the components of the new Creole cuisine. The Spaniards and the indigenous people were deeply scornful and distrustful of each other where food was concerned. For the Europeans maize was always an inferior food, and for the indigenous wheat was a superfluous plant. Collaboration between the two was impossible. The social relation between Europeans and natives was marked by a profound and enduring mutual suspicion.

Something else happened with the Africans. They had prior acquaintance with the Portuguese and the Spanish, having been subjected to slavery since before the discovery of America. From childhood many Africans were sent to Spanish cities and formed in the womb of Hispanic culture. That, for example, is what happened to the Cape Verdean Alonso de Illescas (he adopted his master's name), who landed on the Pacific coast of Esmeraldas, in modern-day Ecuador, and joined the native communities to create the "Zambo Kingdom" of Esmeraldas (*zambo* in Spanish means an African Amerindian hybrid), where Afro-descendants gained their freedom earlier than in any other part of America.

The Esmeraldan experience is fundamental to understanding the process of the creation of the culture of the Colombian Pacific, especially its culinary culture, but this is not the time to recount that epic. I refer my reader to my chronicle, published in the book *Rutas de libertad: Quinientos años de travesía* (Routes of freedom: Five hundred years of crossing) under the title of "El estado natural de la libertad" (The natural state of freedom).[5] Very briefly, in the Cauca Valley region, slaves were sent to work in the mines and jungle areas, places remote from haciendas and villages, where they entered into contact with surviving groups of Native Americans. In the mining areas and the periphery of the haciendas, on the margins of colonial society, the exchanges between Afro-descendants and natives took place. For the first black slaves, those jungle regions were unknown, and they learned from the indigenous to take shortcuts through the forest, to distinguish poisonous plants from edibles, to use the poisonous ones for hunting or fishing, to prepare unfamiliar foods, and even to convoke strange spirits. Everything necessary for life they obtained from the indigenous and, of course, in the case of black women, every way to prepare food.

In that way tamales, cornmeal griddle cakes, all manner of beverages (orig.: *chuyaco*), plants, and spices passed from the table of the native people to that of the black people, and from there to the table of the white people.[6] In the opposite direction the Iberian homemaker's knowledge was assimilated by black cooks and from them it was passed on to indigenous women. The Afro-descendant woman came to play a pivotal role in the process of transculturation. It was in her hands that racial mixing happened, and from those hands the process fanned out to encompass society at large. Of course, she added her own two cents, as her mind was not a blank sheet of paper. This is a peculiarity in the process of formation of culinary culture in the Cauca Valley region: strictly speaking, without the African component there would not be a Cauca Valley cuisine to speak of, nor would there be a regional culture. But defending this type of assertion would require another whole book, for which reason I should stop now and let the reader take over.

All that is left for me to do is recall a birthday luncheon to which my daughter recently treated me: rice with coconut and spinach, Creole-style beef tongue—swimming in a sauce made of garlic, onions, sweet chili pepper, and ripe tomato and sprinkled with chopped cilantro—and two *aborrajados*, crunchy and salted dough on the outside and dripping with ripe plantain syrup within. For dessert we had Cauca Valley *bienmesabe* (literally "tastes good to me"), which is one of the most delicate and extraordinary custards extant.[7]

This is a menu from *Black Cookstove*. It is the product of an ancient dance. Blacks, whites, and Indians dance to the sound of the beautiful voices of Afro-Colombian women. These are the fruits of transculturation, the taste of racial mixing, the beauty of the impure. I have been so fortunate as to enjoy these fruits all my life, much as I am enjoying thinking about and writing these prefatory comments.

GERMÁN PATIÑO OSSA

MAP OF "CAUCA COUNTRY" IN SOUTHWEST COLOMBIA

· · · · · · · · · · · · · · · · · · · ·

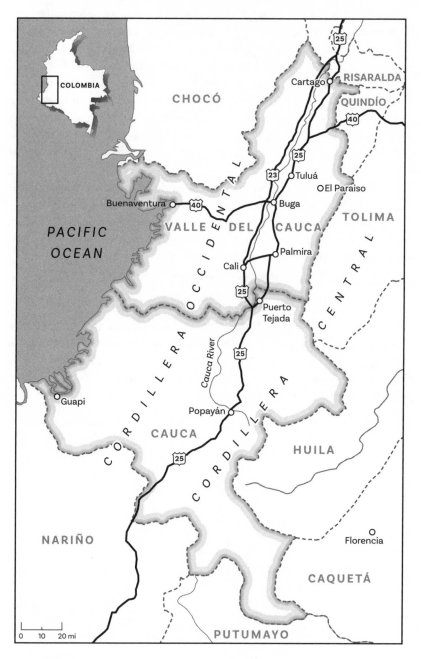

Germán Patiño Ossa's *Black Cookstove: Meditations on Literature, Culture, and Cuisine in Colombia* is my first translation of a nonfiction text, after having translated six Spanish American novels into English. Not especially metaphorical in its style or complex in its sentence structure, it is not the most linguistically difficult work I have confronted. Rather, it is a welcoming, marvelously synthetic essay, not requiring specialized training, on a very basic topic: food and its place in human culture. Its thesis—that Cauca Valley culture is inextricably African at its root—does put a rather fine point on that basic topic, though, as official Colombian culture has long insisted on the purity of its Iberian pedigree. The African element, not only its presence but its catalytic, facilitating, empowering role in Latin America's evolution toward its present form, is something that has fascinated me and driven my scholarship—that is, my continuing education—since I realized I was a Latin Americanist.

No wonder, then, that my first literary translation, begun in 1976, was an Afro-Ecuadorian novel, titled *Juyungo* and written by the self-identified mulatto Adalberto Ortiz. The first thing I learned from carrying out that translation was that getting published was both uncertain and potentially lengthy. It was not until 1982 that *Juyungo* saw the light of day, and that was only thanks to a very dedicated editor-publisher named Donald Herdeck, whose Three Continents Press specialized in the niche of works that somehow thematically linked the Americas with Africa. The novel, intriguing stylistically for its mixing of socialist-realist and modernist techniques, tells the tale of an Afro-Ecuadorian who, through a series of conflicts, armed and otherwise, grows from a consciousness whose parameters are initially racial to an awareness of belonging to a worldwide class struggle. The term *juyungo*, applied to the novel's protagonist, is highly charged regionally, meaning "black man," "monkey," or "devil" in the language of the Cayapas. But those senses could not possibly be conveyed in the title without violating the text's carefully constructed aesthetics. Before even starting to treat the corpus of the novel, then, I realized that, owing to the incompatibilities between two or more subaltern cultures, I could not avoid incurring the fabled loss inherent in translation.

Other valuable lessons awaited me in my next two translation projects, both of novels by the Afro-Colombian writer, considered by many to be the dean of all Afro-Hispanic narrators, Manuel Zapata Olivella. By the time I met Manuel, in 1984, I was a declared Colombianista, having fallen in love with the country and its people through several research trips there. This meant that I was a scholar dedicated to the study of Colombian literature and culture and, through my interest in Manuel's work, also an Afro-colombianista. Perhaps because of my previous translation of *Juyungo* (this was never said explicitly), Manuel offered me the opportunity to translate his epic saga of the African diaspora in the Americas, *Changó, el Gran Putas* (later translated as *Changó, the Biggest Badass*), a vast and immensely complicated combination of history and myth, prose and poetry, Western and non-Western thought, which had been published in Spanish the year before. Feeling woefully inadequate to confront such an undertaking, I asked if he had anything more modest on which I could cut my translator's teeth. He suggested *Chambacú, corral de negros* (*Chambacú, Black Slum*), a relatively straightforward novel of social protest set in a miserably poor district on the outskirts of Cartagena, and I gratefully accepted.

Looking back on the process of translating that novel, I recall gaining a growing appreciation for the narrative's staccato and muscular, Hemingwayesque prose, entirely appropriate to the novel's theme of resistance, both political and existential. But where I learned the most was in the sphere of the cultural, for Afro-Colombia is not the same as Afro-Ecuador. The Atlantic (the setting of *Chambacú*) is not the Pacific. Colombia did not wage war against Peru in the twentieth century, as did Ecuador. But it did participate in the Korean War, with all the damage, both physical and psychological, one might expect from such violence, as the plot plausibly relates. In fact, it was the specifics of the Afro-Colombian experience—the precise geography, mix of races and ethnicities, role of the Catholic Church, role of the government, exposure to US investment and influence, range of diction, and drugs of choice—that contributed to my development as a more competent agent of cultural dissemination.

Once *Chambacú* was a reality (in 1989), I felt that my apprenticeship was sufficient to the task of translating a magnum opus like *Changó*. I have already characterized it as an epic saga of the African diaspora in the Americas. What is initially awe inspiring about *Changó* is its immense span in both space and time. Set in eight different locales (West Africa, the Atlantic Ocean, Venezuela, Colombia, Haiti, Brazil, Mexico, and the United States) across a span of five centuries (the sixteenth to the twentieth), *Changó* provides powerful examples of the evils of the African slave trade organized by a loose consortium of European powers at the dawn of modernity. This well-known history is cast, quite uniquely, as the fulfillment of a curse issued by Changó, the Yoruban orisha of fire, thunder, and war. Wrathful for having been cast out of the pantheon of his fellow gods, Changó condemns the African peoples to a fate of homeless wandering that will, counterintuitively, eventuate in the redeeming freedom of all humanity.

Having managed to get past the novel's monumental dimensions, however, I came upon the true challenge this text embodies: conveying the text's non-Western worldview, whereby the characters, sometimes historical, other times legendary-mythical, go about their lives conversing with their sacred ancestors, beings that hover like somber clouds above their heads. In this unfamiliar world, where the past and the present constantly interact, linear time is out of the question, a consideration that presents extraordinary challenges to any translator. Sentences, consequently, may be composed of a jumble of tenses, spanning variants on the past, present, and future, making for a bumpy ride in Spanish, and no less so in English (the bumps may appear in different places, though). Daring to carry out this project was a sort of trial by fire, perhaps the ultimate test of a translator's willingness to risk utter failure.

I did not know of the existence of *Fogón de negros* [*Black Cookstove* in its original] until 2008, when it was brought to my attention by Professor Darío Henao Restrepo, the dean of humanities at the Universidad del Valle, in Cali. It was apparent on the book's cover that it had won two international awards, although, having participated in several book-award juries, I knew that awards can be political and in themselves are no guarantee of quality. A quick first read of the text, however, convinced me that this should be my next project. I was ready to take on something new, just so long as it wasn't anything on the order of *Changó*. Without my knowing it at the time, my preparation for undertaking the Colombian historian Germán Patiño Ossa's extended essay was all but complete. My knowledge of Afro-Colombian history, literature, religion, psychology, and language had developed and improved with each successive exercise. All I needed was to expand my vocabulary in the realm of the kitchen, and the book would practically translate itself. Not so.

Now I must ask myself, why choose *Black Cookstove*? The act of selecting a text for translation is never innocent. I cannot imagine undertaking the difficult—if pleasurable—task of rendering a document in another language unless there is some sort of affinity between the author and the translator. Whether the concordance is ideological, aesthetic, or something much murkier, the translator must, to some degree, want to participate in extending the source text's reach into the target language and culture. The case of *Black Cookstove* is no exception to that rule. As I mentioned, my very first impression upon reading it was that it needed to be known to readers not only beyond the region of the Cauca River Valley, whose cuisine it studies, but also beyond the book's national and linguistic boundaries.

The degree of my enthusiasm over a booklet of such modest proportions lies, I think, precisely in those proportions: rarely does one find a study of such broad multidisciplinary reach—encompassing the fundamentals of cooking, kitchens, the division of labor, climate, native flora and fauna, hunting, fishing, farming, hospitality, slavery, and literary realism, as well as the links between these elements (in sum, of culture)—in so compact, clear-spoken, and generally accessible a bundle.

Among the features I find compelling in this essay are, first, the fact that Patiño Ossa's study focuses not on the capital region of Bogotá (which features a fertile and productive savannah) but rather on a district that lies far from the nation's center, in its southwest periphery. In addition to its central role in Colombia's politics, Bogotá, with its relatively high altitude (roughly 8,000 feet, in contrast to the Cauca Valley's roughly 3,300 feet), makes for a very different environment (cool and rainy, or cool and sunny), and the story of its regional cuisine and culture would also have been very different. Second, in the Cauca Valley region, during the period of legal slavery (not ended until 1851), Afro-descendants were, in general, poor in every sense—especially in their freedom—but not in their diet. Contrary to the conventional assumption of ubiquitous misery and hunger, the region's natural abundance—its fertile soil, teeming waters, tropical forests, and abundant rainfall—was such that, unless a master wanted to punish a given slave through starvation, there was always more than enough food to go around.

Third, this study features the deployment of a startling strategy: the use of Romantic fiction—the novel *María* (1867), by Jorge Isaacs—as a realistic yardstick to gauge social practices characteristic of the place and time: class and race differences, intrafamilial relations, the use of food as a tool of seduction, and so on. A fourth and very pleasant insight resides in the book's enlightening lesson that Afro-descendant women, in controlling the community's food supply, occupied an immensely powerful and even transformative position in Creole society. Not only did these women feed their masters and everyone on their farms and ranches, or villages, they also enacted the hybridization of cooking and culture among the region's Iberian, indigenous, and African sources. Fifth, I would signal the deeply universal humanity of the region's inhabitants conveyed in this multidisciplinary analysis of the inseparability of cooking and culture. It does not hurt, additionally, that the book includes rare illustrations, some from as far back as the 1830s, which complement and enrich the verbal treatment of its subject matter. And finally, for now, this text represents an attempt—successful, by my lights—at vindicating a people that have suffered displacement and enslavement; a loss of their possessions and native language, their gods, and their identities; and an endless series of unspeakable injustices but who still remain proud, unbowed, and creative. Surely these and other qualities were paramount in the minds of the juries that awarded *Fogón de negros* the prestigious international prizes it has garnered. It is, quite simply, a gem of an essay, and an example of unpretentious but solid scholarship well worth emulating.

Every text presents its translator with special challenges. In this case the challenges were almost exclusively nominal—that is, related to naming. Because names, outside of onomatopoeia, have an arbitrary relation with the objects to which they refer, translating the popular name of a plant, animal, or dish from

FIG. 1 Capybara (*Hydrochoerus hydrochaeris*) at Zona Brazil exhibit at Bristol Zoo, 2014

one language to another may not get us any closer to understanding the object being named. If, for example, the original text refers to a leaf called *paico*, and we find that its equivalent in English is "wormwood," and if we do not know the properties associated with that thing (its color, shape, taste, texture, effect on the skin or gastrointestinal tract, etc.), substituting one name for another is not especially helpful. (In fact, wormwood is a purgative used to eliminate roundworm parasites.) If, in addition, we are talking about a species of animal or plant that has no equivalent in other, climatologically distinct parts of the world, such as the large rodent locally called a *chigüiro* (known more universally as *capybara*, not quite a household name but, I am told, a succulent dish), the problem is even more acute (see fig. 1).

I have tried to address such problems in any of three different ways. First, in the case of culturally unique phenomena—such as the protean dish called *fufú* (an explanation of which appears later in the essay)—I have incorporated into the narrative as much descriptive information as possible. Second, when such description is inadequate, I have resorted to Carl Linnaeus's traditional binomial nomenclature (the scientific genus and species in Latin). And, third, when added descriptions or binomial nomenclature would have excessively complicated the essay's economical, streamlined prose, I have inserted an endnote in the narrative and provided explanatory material outside the primary text. But where exactly does the line lie between excessive complication and acceptable elaboration in producing a linguistic and cultural translation? The results of dealing with this and so many other conundrums are never perfect, and the goal of rendering the source text with complete transparency remains for me an unsated hunger.

¡Buen apetito!

JONATHAN TITTLER

Camden, NJ—Cali, Colombia—Remsen, NY, 2009–20

PREAMBLE
Tale of a Voyage

Introduction

Between 1823 and 1825 the British government envoy, Col. John P. Hamilton, traveled through the provinces of Colombia, a country that had recently completed its Wars of Independence, was devastated by losses, and had its economy in ruins. Despite all that, he had the opportunity to be pleasantly surprised, particularly in the Greater Cauca region, where he was treated with the greatest courtesy, as if he were the lord mayor of London.

The foods that Hamilton ate—the meals he shared and the smells and flavors that fascinated him—were the product of three centuries of transculturation,[1] a multiethnic stew that was a blend of pre-Hispanic, Hispanic, and Afro-descendant culinary wisdom, creating a unique tropical cuisine, where rivers and meadows, winds, ardent summers, and eternal snows mixed. It was a cuisine of abundance, traditional and exotic, replete with unexpected combinations, a barely glimpsed, forgotten feast that, almost despite itself, provided an undercurrent for the Latin American way of being in those regions of great environmental diversity and imposed slavery.

In Popayán, amid the multiple receptions and tributes, some of which featured Spanish wines forty years in the aging, which the affected Englishman could not enjoy because he found them "too sweet and heavy," he was surprised on two occasions, to which he dedicates special attention in his memoirs. On the first occasion, at the bishop's home, he remembers that "the feast was what one might expect for a bishop. . . . Fish and fruit were served that I had never seen before, and all these exquisite victuals were copiously irrigated with aged Malaga, as well as other Spanish wines."[2]

Although no mention is made of it, the banquet must have begun with some sort of soup or perhaps with some portions of fufú, mentioned in Jorge Isaacs's

FIG. 2 A. Faguet, *Assorted Fruit*, 1869

María, which was green plantain dough cooked in a hearty broth, perhaps a reduction made of the juices of the fish to be served as the main dish.[3] The Malaga, if we are to believe Dumas, must have been made by confectioners and would be reminiscent of a muscatel, but maybe not as sweet as those aged wines that were too strong for Colonel Hamilton's palate, for on that occasion he voiced no complaint.[4] Dionisio Pérez, in *Guía del buen comer español* (Guide to good Spanish eating), confirms for us this appreciation in suggesting that the older Malagas were elaborated by using raisins as a starter.[5]

Fish with fruit? With fruit "I had never seen before," meaning tropical fruit. This starts to look like the fare of contemporary auteur cuisine or of ancient Asian dinners, but it was served at the most traditional of Cauca tables, that of the bishop, in the most traditional of New Granada's cities, Popayán, and in 1823, no less. It should not strike us as strange, then, as we shall see later, that in a normal home in the Cauca Valley countryside, the meal would revolve around a dish of fish with fruit. Further back, almost a century before, a Dominican priest given to fine dining had been caught serving a combination of shellfish and green papaya salad.[6] For Mr. Hamilton, who was chary in praise, those were "exquisite victuals."

Not having yet recuperated from this delicate offering, in a most singular event, he and his assistant were hosted by Carmelite nuns—who were known to go to great pains to set a good table—and were served, as a jewel of their cook-stove, a turtle soup that, it was later known, was prepared by a black novitiate with a "most beautiful voice for song." The grave Englishman lost his composure and confessed, without regret, that he had three servings of that "delicacy."[7] The colonel's secretary, a young man whose name does not matter, suffered unimag-ined effects from the soup and slipped away during a momentary lapse in the vigilance of the mother superior, who later found him in a forbidden place and in animated conversation with the attractive novitiate. Mr. Hamilton hastened to offer embarrassed apologies and then wrote stern reflections on the short-comings in character of the new generation of British youth.

At some time before, other young people—Creoles who at that time were in their eighties—gave testimony to the consistently high quality of the cuisine proper to the geographic valley of the Cauca River. One of the reasons why the cattle drives from Florida to Palmira were unforgettable was the routine stop at a farmhouse on the banks of the Bolo River, beyond Pradera, where the black cooks were always at the ready to serve the cowboys fragrant casseroles of turtle soup, accompanied by toasted plantains and white rice, which was washed down with a burning carafe of *aguardiente* (brandy), sometimes distilled on the prem-ises, in the clandestine stills that have continuously existed since the advent of sugarcane in the Cauca Valley in the sixteenth century.[8] About the effects of the stimulating soup on the temperament of those other young people of the decade of the 1940s we will not comment, for the mulatto population sprinkled about those parts provides the best documentation possible in this regard.

But fish and turtles as main dishes in the Popayán of the early nineteenth century—especially if, as Hamilton himself noted, the Cauca and its tributaries in the Pubenza Valley were poor for fishing, owing to the acidity of rivers such as the Vinagre and the sulfurous springs that fed the streams? Fish and turtle were served for two reasons: because it was a matter of meals for special occa-sions and because, farther north, in the greater Cauca River Valley, that river and its tributaries served as a veritable emporium of piscene and amphibian riches, however difficult that may be for us to imagine today.

As to the first point, it was the intention of the bishop and the mother superior to serve His Majesty's envoy something special, something that they themselves considered proper to singular occasions. This is a cultural trait that still bedevils us. A certain inferiority complex and the idea that the foreign—ideally the European—is better than all the rest, and especially better than our own, are relevant characteristics of the Latin American cultural universe, espe-cially among the upper classes.

They could just as well have surprised him with a tasty squash tamale, or a *carantanta* (corn-based) soup, or with Creole-style ground beef, all of these swim-ming in chili-spiced peanuts and, of course, accompanied by numerous fruits, among which would stand out, and still does, the custard apple.[9] But, just like the custard or fritters that Isaacs mentions in his novel *María*, this other menu was too popular, in a manner of speaking, too commonplace. It was necessary to take recourse to what was not within just anyone's reach, a quality that speaks to the buying power of the homeowners, their influence—noteworthy in the case of the bishop—and their effort to recognize the important guest, serving him what was out of the ordinary. That explains, for instance, the aged Malaga wines, which they could have done without, replacing them with a freshly fermented *masato de chontaduro* (sweet dessert wine)—the best of all, according to Friar Juan de Santa Gertrudis—or with a soursop sorbet.[10] As the seventeenth-century Spaniard Francisco de Quevedo y Villegas wrote in verse, "It is not the fish you eat, but the fame, / the cost, and the exotic, which are prized."[11]

Regarding the second point, they in any case had at hand the fish and turtles native to the Cauca River Valley. The truth is that these fish and amphibian dishes were fare produced by the region's black women well before that of the *ñapangas* (mixed Spanish and indigenous young ladies) of the Pubenza Valley, where the city of Popayán is located. They could not have come from the Pacific coast because the distance to Guapi and Timbiquí is great, rendering it impossible for the fish to arrive in an acceptably fresh condition. Popayán's elite, eager to impress the British ambassador, had a tradition of fine dining and knew that a splendid platter of seafood depended entirely on its being the same day's catch. Even today, despite all the advances in refrigeration and food preservation, that ancient truth still stands.

Understanding this situation takes us back to a more remote past, to the beginnings of our peculiar process of racial mixing.[12] The exact date was Saint Michael's Day of 1540, which is to say, September 29. That morning in Vijes, New Granada (later, Colombia), on fifteen bamboo rafts, or broad reeds, as the Spaniards called them, Jorge Robledo and his troop, a few black slaves, and Indian servants embarked on the first documented navigation of the Cauca River. It was a true voyage of exploration, lasting two weeks and ending in a tumultuous shipwreck at the rapids just beyond Sopinga, near today's La Virginia, in the present-day province of Risaralda. The chronicle of this expedition has been preserved; it is one of the most colorful of the Spanish Conquest, penned by the scribe Juan Bautista Sardella.[13]

It is of interest that the Spaniards truly suffered, especially from hunger, as they did not carry sufficient provisions. To the Afro-descendants who accompanied them, this world was just as unknown, and the Indian servants either were Yanaconas brought by Sebastián de Belalcázar—in which case they also found themselves on unfamiliar terrain—or were waiting for both the whites and the blacks to die so that they could flee into the jungle.[14] Hunting in the clearings of the enormous bamboo groves that covered both banks of the Cauca River was an

FIG. 3 A. de Neuville, *Young Mestiza Women of the Cauca Valley*, 1869

exact science at which they failed: the fish of the Cauca were not easily hooked, the turtles appeared only at certain intervals and almost always at night, and the playful *agoutis* were slippery water dwellers that brought sweat to the brow of even the most experienced hunters.

Fortunately, after several days' suffering, they met some natives who "came with meals of corn, yucca, and fish, of which there was very great need," according to Sardella's narrative. This is the basis for food and eating in the Cauca Valley, not only in that period but also for at least the first century of colonization. It is true that soon would come along the banana, already known to the

Africans, and rice (Asian but also cultivated and enjoyed especially by the Africans), which would be essential to the diet, above all in regions where slaves abounded. But "corn, yucca, and fish" would form an essential tripod basic to the traditional cuisine of the Greater Cauca region.[15]

The fishing was so abundant that it exceeded their nutritional needs. The natives who helped Jorge Robledo were, according to Pedro Cieza de León, the Gorrón Indians, thus called

> because when in the valley they established the city of Cali, they named the fish *gorrón*. . . . They came loaded with them, saying, "gorrón, gorrón." . . . These Indians live at some distance from the valley and the main river (Cauca), at two and three and four leagues, and at the appropriate times they would go down to the lagoons and that main river, whence they would return with a great quantity of fish. . . . They kill an infinite number of tasty fish, which they give to the travelers and sell them in the cities of Cartago and Cali and elsewhere. . . . They have large warehouses of them dried to sell and great jugs filled with lard, which they get from the fish. . . . This province of the gorrones is very abundant in corn and other things.[16]

Fresh fish, very tasty, large deposits of dried fish, large jugs of fish lard: that is the main source of protein for nutrition and the foundation of the traditional cuisine of the Cauca Valley, as well as of the fat for the African slaves' fried dishes and, of course, the base for Spanish stews.

Our regional cuisine, simmered during several centuries of racial mixing, was fully formed before the end of the colonial period. And in that cooking one always finds, among many other things, an abundance of fish, amphibians, and aquatic mammals in the Cauca River Valley, not to mention the Pacific coast, in easy contact with Cali as of 1539. Some testimonials, gathered shortly before the start of the Wars of Independence (1808–9), would remind us of a good part of the forgotten banquet feast.[17]

Don Cayetano Núñez, district mayor of Riofrío during that same period, tells us that the locals dedicated themselves, among other activities, "to catching fish, for in the Main River there are *bocachico* [literally "cute mouth"], *jetudo* [big snout], catfish, and shad, the fishing of which is accomplished with hooks, nets, and harpoons."[18] Don Pedro José de Soto, in charge of the town of Yunde, on the highway that today connects Cali to Candelaria, informs us of "the catching of medium-size fish produced in the marshes associated with the Cauca River: the name of this fish in general is bocachico, which they catch by hook or net." Don Pedro José Guerrero, from Jamundí, notes that "of the aforementioned Jamundí River, where fish abound, the most exquisite, among which are the *barbudo* [bearded one, *Pimelodus blochi*], shad, sardine, *jetudo*, *rayado* [striper], *sabaleta* [small shad, *Brycon henni*], along with the most common which they call bocachico, are caught in the upper reaches and are of extremely delicate taste."[19] Don Luis de Vergara, the city attorney for Cali in that same postindependence war period, reports, "fishing, in the lagoons of the Cauca River, with various sorts of nets at their respective peak seasons, produces by the hundreds what are called bocachicos, an ordinary fish that sustains the poor people; and *veringo* [literally "naked one"], a species of scaleless *aquil*; catfish; barbudo; *sardinata* [*Pellona castelneana*]; and shad, which are all appreciated. . . . Also common are capybara, otter, muskrat, turtle, iguana—all water-dwellers."

These testimonials should suffice, for they are repeated with few variations throughout the whole territory, as far as Cartago. Food was so abundant that the physician Evaristo García, at the start of the twentieth century, complained of the laziness of the Cauca Valley mulattos, for it was enough to cut a bunch of bananas, which grew wild, and to toss out one's net, to take care of the family's needs for the day, with a surplus for any guests.[20] Then one would go off to make *aguardiente* in the still that was hidden in the bamboo thicket. That is the source of all the parties, the numerous children, and "so many unruly darkies."

Besides all this, there was the port of Buenaventura and the rivers that flowed into the Pacific, which like a magnet attracted landowners from the Cauca Valley and from Popayán for their riches in gold, and Buenaventura was the only place to engage in trade with the outside world. Through that port would pass European liquors, conserves, salt, sometimes wheat flour, olive oil, and, to be sure, coconut products. Of course, there were also more fish of other varieties, shellfish and crustaceans, and abundant meat from aquatic mammals, among other things.

Of those water dwellers, other than the freshwater turtle, whose soup we have already discussed, another animal stands out for its delicate meat and caught the attention of Mr. Hamilton. When he reached Buga, after his stay in Popayán, he wrote that "one finds in the great lake near the city the *agouti*, an otter-like mammal of darkish color with white markings on its sides. . . . The meat of this animal is in high demand."[21] It was, to the utmost degree, and with good reason. Its meat is lean and delicious, and it can be prepared in a variety of ways. It was so coveted that the peasants of the Cauca Valley figured out how to raise *agoutis* in captivity, notwithstanding the technical difficulties of maintaining enclosures of woven bamboo through which fresh water could circulate. The *agouti* can still occasionally be found in the rivers of the Pacific, and it is a special occasion to consume it in a splendid stew, in which the delicate meat cooks over a low fire, simmering in abundant coconut water.

Despite the growth of agribusiness and the consequent contamination of our waters, which have extinguished the unimaginable abundance and variety of the fisheries, the tradition still survives among the common people. Black cooks continue to prepare bocachico soup or steamed catfish. Different varieties of fried fish, prepared on outdoor cookstoves, with toasted banana chips and fresh *lulo* juice, constitute a breakfast that is greatly appreciated by the sand diggers of Juanchito, the stevedores of Cavasa, or the porters of Jamundí.[22] The same meal is enjoyed in the evenings as well, but without the *lulo* juice, by exhausted pairs of dancers decked out in multicolored costumes. This ancestral taste for diverse seafood has expressed itself from the Ecuadorian coast to Buenaventura in the popular consumption of shrimp ceviche, which is sold everywhere, from market stands and supermarkets to portable kitchen carts. Its poor cousins, smoked baby shark and canned tuna ceviche—both highly recommended—also please the popular palate.

The "exquisite victuals" that in 1823 the British ambassador was accorded, if indeed not common fare in the noble city, were therefore part of the daily cuisine of the mulatto folks who dwelled in the northern part of the province of Popayán. The routine consumption of different species of fish was an integral part of the new Creole culture and was attributable to the abundance in natural resources.

But then, just a few days later, between Cali and Palmira, upon dining at the hacienda El Bolo, he finds that "we were served a meal combined in the most curious of ways: first the soup, then a plate of vegetables, followed by beef and fruit, and then sweets and cheese."[23] In the land of the turtle, the fish, and the *agouti*, instead of them all: beef. We again find a combination that seems to be of our own time: meat and fruit—plus cheese, a combination that requires a healthy dairy industry. But in those days nothing came from outside the region. By then the territory of the Cauca River Valley had been transformed into the largest livestock emporium in the country's collective memory.

Then Came Pigs and Cattle

Cultural nostalgia of the most powerful sort, that pertaining to the taste buds, led the Spaniards who settled the Cauca Valley to spend fortunes in the early days to bring to their tables a pork shoulder or nice cut of beef loin. Cieza de León reports in the decade of the 1540s that when the conquistador Cristóbal de Ayala died, in Buga, his goods were sold at extravagant prices, "because a sow was sold for 1,600 pesos, along with another pig, and small pigs were sold at 500. . . . I saw that the same sow was eaten one day when there was a banquet . . . and Juan Pacheco, a conquistador who is now in Spain, sold a pig for 225 pesos. . . . From the wombs of the sows one could buy, before they were born, the suckling pigs for 100 pesos or more."[24]

Very soon thereafter Sebastián de Belalcázar brought cattle from Peru, and pigs and cows began to thrive in Greater Cauca, from Pasto in the south to

FIG. 4
E. Riou, *Flooded
Pine-Nut Swamp,*
1875–76

Cartago in the north. From the visits paid by an anonymous author between 1559 and 1560, and then in 1582 by Friar Gerónimo de Escobar, we find documentation of growth in the livestock population of the entire region.[25] The anonymous author says of Popayán, "The houses of the Spaniards are generally made of adobe walls, and they are covered with tiles. They raise all types of livestock, cows, sheep, goats, and mares, and the best horses to be found in the Indies are from that city and from Cali." "Livestock" in this case means pigs—that is, herds of swine. Of Cali, in turn, it is reported that "the Spaniards of that city raise large quantities of swine, sheep, goats, mares, and cows, and there are wonderful conditions for all that." The swine were raised free range, pastured, in great herds that were led to the bottomland of the Cauca Valley so that they could feed on the pine nuts produced by the *burilico* (*Xylopia calophylla*) tree.

FIG. 5 Valette, *Fettered Pigs Near Popayán*, 1875–76

As it was not cost-effective to raise boars, just a few males were selected as sires, the most robust and hardiest stock, while the others were sacrificed between fifteen and twenty days after birth, to complement the fare of the forgotten banquet feast. Raising pigs was most popular, since it was within the reach of poor peasants, mulattos and freed slaves alike. Many eyewitness accounts exist in that regard. Quickly slaves and settlers learned to roast suckling pig in a simple fashion, as it was done in Castile. An old recipe, as presented by Dionisio Pérez, conveys the idea:

> The animal is chosen between fifteen and twenty days of age. It is slaughtered and completely immersed in a cauldron of boiling water. Once it is nice and clean and white, cut open a channel the length of the belly, from the snout to the tail. Remove all entrails and wash again inside and out, wiping thoroughly with burlap. Stretch it out as if it were a tanned hide and run a barbecue spit along its entire length, while not allowing the cavity to close. With a swab moistened in brine, daub and moisten all over and expose it to a glowing charcoal fire, rotating continuously. With each turn, rub it with a slice of good bacon, and afterward moisten it with the brine until the skin blisters and takes on the color of a hazelnut. An hour and a half should suffice for the entire operation. Bacon is preferred to lard because the former softens as it cooks, while the latter makes the skin crunchy.[26]

FIG. 6 Bayard, *A Farm in Tropical Climes*, 1869

This is traditional cuisine, simple and exquisite. This delicacy was consumed by the guests at the wedding banquet of Doña Inés de Lara, at the Cañasgordas Estate, as Eustaquio Palacios recounts in his novel *El alférez real* (The royal second lieutenant). The same applies as well to an enormous stuffed sow, among many other things, but Eugenio Barney Cabrera has already told that story in his indispensable essay on Cauca Valley cuisine.[27] Here we are interested in showing the abundance of traditional cooking, replete with long-lost subtleties. This roast suckling pig was not an aristocratic dish but rather one of common access to all, rich and poor, like the turtle soup and the fish and meat with fruits.

Something else was happening. The climate, the fertility of the soil in the bottomland of the tributaries and rivers, the variety of legumes and grasses, and the broad meadows and pastures of the valley brought about a breathtaking growth in the number of head of cattle. This was true to such a point that, at the beginning of the eighteenth century, there were already large landowners and livestock breeders the whole length of the Cauca Valley. On the visit of Manuel de Abastas and Francisco Javier Torijano in 1721, for example, it is reported how 1,000 cows grazed at the estate of Gregorio de Zúñiga in Dominguillo, just as at Francisco de Arboleda's in Quilachao, and another 1,200 in the Jesuit property of Japio.[28] The largest owner was Nicolás de Caicedo, with 17,000 head of cattle on Las Animas Estate between Cartago and Buga. But there were also others, like Domingo Cobo, who had 8,565 head at Bugalagrande; Francisco Olano, with 4,000 at Los Chancos; and Salvador de Caicedo at the Cali commons with more than 3,000. Hundreds of proprietors owned more than 100 head, and large herds of maverick livestock grazed in the northern stretches of the valley and along other frontiers. According to John P. Hamilton, before the Wars of Independence, the Cauca River Valley supported a million head of cattle, and enormous cattle drives flooded the markets of Antioquia, Bogotá, Popayán, and even Quito, in Ecuador.

That explains the everyday abundant presence of meat, milk, and dairy products on the tables of Cauca Valley families. Meat would be prepared in a multitude of ways: fresh, salted, and sun-dried; salted and smoked; combined with fruits, as Hamilton tasted it; in a *sancocho*; shredded and conserved in *hogao*; barbecued with *pintones* (semiripe plantains); ground up and pickled; steamed with potatoes and yucca; smoked and then fried; oven-baked in a pastry or as meatballs; in a fricassee, "very tender and better than the way it is prepared in New York," as Isaac Holton confirmed in 1852; in steaks Creole style and under fried eggs; not to mention liver, tongue, and brisket, tripe, beef hocks, shanks, tails with hot chili, stuffed turnovers, and yucca pastries; and in so many other forms that one could go on listing them forever.[29]

In addition to the variety of preparations of beef—remember we also have fish, aquatic mammals, and pigs, plus others of which nothing has been said—there is milk, which enriches the valley's cuisine in many ways. At daybreak in the corral, one would draw milk—ideally from a cow with a large calf—directly into a glass, in which grated unrefined brown sugar with lemon juice is mixed, to obtain *boruga*, a type of warm *kumis* that should be drunk immediately before the whey separates. Some milkmaids would add to the sweet-and-sour base a splash of *aguardiente*, and some landowners, a nip of brandy. It was a nice way to start the day.

Despite the fact that milk would be consumed at all meals, accompanying a mature roast—especially the foamy *postrera*, milked from cows near weaning and preserved in the cool of the stables—or beaten into chocolate, or mixed into dough for cakes, breads, and wraps, when not for *dulce de leche* and rice pudding, there was so much left over that it was necessary to save it in the form of butter and cheese, with as many cheese varieties produced as the climate allowed. Curds, *queso fresco*, cottage cheese, creamy cheese to spread—even a cream cheese made of colostrum milk was produced to serve to children—the stone cheese Isaacs mentions, an elastic cheese derived from cooking rennet in whey, and so on: it would go with *arepa* (corn muffin), wheat bread, a thousand fried dishes, conserves. It would be marinated with onions, garlic, black pepper, herbs, and other condiments; would go hand and glove with sweets; and would form the ideal combination in the simplest and most perfect dessert of

Cauca Valley cuisine: *queso fresco* in sugarcane syrup. It could not be otherwise, coming as it did from the land of livestock husbandry and sugarcane.[30]

All this explains how one could concoct a meal that combined beef with fruit and ended with sweets and cheese, a practice that caught Mr. Hamilton's attention at El Bolo Estate. It wasn't really anything out of the ordinary, but rather everyday fare in the Cauca Valley, among the powerful as well as the humble. Isaacs, in *María* (1867), describes one of these everyday lunches: "To tell the truth, there were no great delicacies at the lunch, but it was known that Emigdio's mother and sisters knew how to present it: the soup made of aromatized *tortilla* with fresh herbs from the garden; fried plantains, shredded beef, and corn-flour buns; the excellent chocolate of the region; stone cheese, bread pudding, and water served in large antique pitchers."[31]

On another occasion also, in the novel, Efraín is served "white and purple masses of corn, green cheese, and roast beef," and, days later, he admires a mulatto woman "roasting half-cured cheese slivers, frying rolls, bringing *pandebono* rolls to a golden brown, and jelling preserves." As can be observed, meat, milk, and cheese go together readily. But other things do as well, and of these we must now speak.

Things from Hither and Yon

One would have to go back to 1540 and keep in mind the meal we have mentioned of corn, yucca, and fish, "of which there was much need." On that expedition the Spaniards also found "some food of tender corn, and melons of the earth, and pumpkin [*Cucurbita maxima*] and yuccas, and yams, which are good-tasting roots." They found honey in abundance everywhere. In Timaná, which formed part of Greater Cauca, they found wild peanuts, cultivated them, and mounted an industry of nougat candy made of honey and peanuts, which they traded in various parts of the region.[32] They discovered wild vanilla, but neither they nor the indigenous knew how to exploit it (this they would later learn from the Aztecs, via the Spanish missionaries and conquistadors). Avocados accompanied them wherever they went, with special notoriety in the Cauca Valley. Cacao, which again neither outsider nor native knew how to consume, would also be spotted in these parts.[33] And they found fruits, in quantities and varieties that were truly alarming. Star apples, pineapples, coconuts, loquats, soursops, custard apples, passion fruits, quinces, hearts of palm, guavas, *guamas* (*Reynosia guama*, a very large bean), pomegranates, mulberries, cherries, and many more, "which for not knowing their names are not listed," it was charmingly said.[34]

The Spaniards also brought their own provisions. Wheat grew well in Pasto, where there was a mill as early as 1542, to the point that "already in that city

FIG. 7
E. Riou, *Sugarcane Juice*,
1875–76

one does not eat corn bread, because of the abundance of wheat," as Cieza de
León wrote.[35] It also caught on around Popayán. In the Cauca Valley sugarcane
found a privileged environment in which to prosper. Very soon, in 1548, Andrés
Cobo and his brother were exporting sugar to Panama from their mills located
in Amaime. The Spanish also brought fruits with them, especially citrus, which
flourished in the region. Vineyards and olive groves were less common, for
planting them was prohibited by the Crown, although clandestine plantations
are recorded. And plantains and coconuts would play a major role.

In fact, by the start of the 1540s, as Cieza de León recounts, the bases for
the cuisine of the mixed-race population were set in place:

> In these valleys the Spaniards have their farms or ranches, along with their
> servants. . . . Alongside these farms run many beautiful channels, with which
> they irrigate their plantings. . . . There are many orange trees, limes, lemons,

FIG. 8 E. Riou, *Sugarcane Grinder or Mill*, 1875–76

pomegranates, large plantations of banana trees, and even larger plantations of sugarcane. . . . There are pineapples, guavas and soursops, avocados,
and some small grapes that have an external shell, which are very tasty . . . ,
quinces, plums . . . , melons from Spain and many vegetables from Spain
as well as from this land. Up till now they have not planted wheat. . . . The
city is located a league from the Main River, previously mentioned, abutting a small river of singular waters that spring from the mountains. . . .
All the riverbanks are covered with fresh gardens, where there are always
vegetables and fruits.[36]

Rice would be planted in the environs of Jamundí and, initially, in the marshy
lands of modern-day Guacarí.

More important still, they brought slaves from Africa. And the latter adapted
easily to the climate of the warm valleys of Greater Cauca, to its rivers and its
seaboard. By the end of the colonial period, their population thrived to the point
of constituting a majority of the vast territory of the provincial government of
Popayán. In the census of 1789, transcribed by Francisco de Silvestre, it is indicated that the provincial government had 64,463 inhabitants, among whom over
35,000 were black, 22,979 free and 12,241 slaves.[37] They were concentrated in
the Cauca and Patía Valleys and along the Pacific coast. In these zones the black
women became masters of the kitchen. They set themselves up around what, at
a certain time, was disdainfully called a "black cookstove." They also took charge
of the language, of raising children—white and black—of music and dance, and
sometimes of the ancestral home itself, leaving a deep imprint on the culture of
the region.

That is the source of our fried dishes and, according to Eugenio Barney Cabrera, steamed cooking.[38] Slow cooking, often over a low flame, is more characteristically Spanish. These black women, who in general ran everything, including things culinary, created delicacies derived from plantain, rice, and sugarcane. All our dishes bear an African imprint, sometimes as appetizers and always as tasty side dishes: in the golden and translucent *tostadas* of green plantains and in the *marranitas* that Don Leonardo Tascón described with a certain scorn as "bland paste that the poor people make from roasted mashed green plantain, to which they add cracklings," which he confused with the *sango* from Nariño, and which, of course, is based on plantains that are fried, not baked.[39] When they are done right, they are a truly irresistible gustatory treat. One finds the imprint in yucca pastries, also fried, filled with tangy meat stew; in empanadas made of corn dough filled with appetizing meat stew and potatoes, fried till they are golden brown; in *aborrajados*, crunchy on the outside and dripping with ripe banana syrup inside, in perfect combination with the flavor of fresh cheese; and in corn dumplings, golden and crunchy, which melt in one's mouth.

This is so even in our tamales, which have little to do with the Aztec *tamalli*, except for the linguistic denomination, as also happens with the Cauca Valley *pipián* (a type of savory nonmeat filling for empanadas), which differs vastly from the Mexican version.[40] Although the tamales are made of corn and, sometimes, potato and chili peppers (both pre-Hispanic products), the black influence is found in the banana-leaf wrapper and, especially, in the long cooking in boiling water. Beside the tamale, which is common to several regions of the country with only slight variation, it is beef and pork that would become the fashion in the Cauca Valley, and only later would chicken be added. But the black cooks would produce the very delicate "glistening" variety, diminutive in size, made from batter that is white and soft, with a savory meat filling. The surprising *piangua*, a creation of the Pacific coast—in which coconut water instead of broth is used to thin the dough, and the oyster stew is in coconut cream and *hogao*—would make the difference and produce one of the most exquisite dishes of all Colombian cuisine. There would even be a variant that replaced corn in the dough with green plantain, with curious results.

In the wraps—especially the very delicate ones made with baby corn—most of the ingredients, and in this case the wrapper itself, are indigenous. In the Pacific zone, as usual, they would replace butter with coconut water, to smooth out the corn-flour batter, lending it a special flavor. In these wraps it is the cooking—the mode of preparation—that would bear an African stamp.

The same may be said of our sancocho, although its Hispanic ancestry is also undeniable. Much as the garlic, advancing toward the West, reveals the footprints of the armies of ancient Rome, meat and vegetable stew indicates the routes of the Spanish sailors and conquistadors. There would thus be Canary

Islands stew, Cuban stew, Puerto Rican stew, Mexican, Chilean, Peruvian, and so on, which would take the classic names of *puchero*, *cazuela*, and sancocho in Colombia, Puerto Rico, Ecuador, and so on.[41] These stews are modifications of the old *olla podrida* (literally "rotten pot") of Castile, according to the specific foods available in each locale and the people who prepare them. The Cauca Valley version would have its special flair and for a good while it would be made of fish, almost always bocachico, later to be replaced by beef, preferably corned or jerked, although sometimes one might use a cow tail or fresh needlefish. Plantain and yucca were indispensable, and one could add baby corncobs, but never potato or other fillers. Of course, the special taste would depend on the precise combination, the delicate balance among onion, garlic, unsweetened *yerba mate*, and cilantro, which harkens back to the wise old black women cooks. Chicken was served only in exceptional circumstances, and even at that only among the powerful. In nineteenth-century Cali it was said, not without a sense of whimsy, that when a poor person ate a chicken, one or the other was sick.

The development of aviculture and the transformation of livestock ranches into sugarcane plantations contributed to the disappearance of the traditional sancochos with which the kitchen maids raised Cauca Valley inhabitants for four centuries, giving way to the lighter and somewhat insipid chicken soup, which is almost always made from a very young chick, fattened with steroids, exposed to artificial lighting twenty-four hours a day, and doped so that it never sleeps, its only concern being to eat.

And weren't these same matrons the ones who worked miracles with our innumerable fruits: juices, sorbets, jellies, guava paste, preserves, candy?[42] The green and refreshing *luladas*, with the fruit chunked and the seeds left in, and the soursop-based *champús*, which, although known also among the black community of Cartagena, as Friar Juan de Santa Gertrudis tells it, survived only in the Cauca Valley.[43] They combined these fruits with fish, as we have seen, as well as with meats, although the details of those concoctions have been lost. And they were made invariably with cheese or other dairy products, for it should not be forgotten that many of those Africans came, just as did the Spanish, from societies dedicated to raising and grazing milk-producing livestock.

We have read of these mulatto women browning *pandebonos*, frying rolls, and kneading yucca bread. We would see them beating dulce de leche in large copper frying pans, preparing angel hair for Holy Week, candying limes and oranges, shaping corn muffins and the exquisite batter of tender corn. Even the *arepas* acquired a distinctive character, for the bakers would be sure to use high-quality cheese and to make them almost a meal in themselves. They would enrich their menus with multiple soups—too many to enumerate—and would invent a casserole of green beans and tender corn that should be more widely renowned than it is.[44] One of their culinary glories would be, however, rice. They would prepare it in many ways, among which stand out the risotto-like *atollado*, which should have a creamy texture, and rice pudding, always thick, which can be sipped, hot or cold, and which goes well, if one is so inclined, with honey or blackberries in nectar, especially when it curdles just as you dig into it with a spoon.[45] But, above all, they would achieve perfection with white rice, which glistens, prepared so that it crunches between the teeth, even when completely cooked, with its grains separated in such a way that they can be counted one by one. When made with coconut, it is a culinary achievement that lends itself to a plethora of variants.

Of course, racial mixing alone was not enough. Even though the precise hybridization of Europeans with Africans, over a native bed of embers, has produced varied, exquisite, and singular cuisines, as happens with the Cajun and Creole cooking of the Mississippi Delta or the Bahian kitchen and that of certain parts of northeast Brazil, time and a diversity of raw materials were required, and no habitat is as amenable to such needs as the Cauca River Valley.

Our traditional cuisine arose as part of the new Creole (uniquely American, as opposed to peninsular Spanish) culture that took shape through a long process whose roots reach back to the period of Spanish domination. It is a sister of Creole literature, which begins to form in *El carnero* (The sheepskin), by Juan Rodríguez Freyle; of music, which achieves its most definitive form in the *bambuco viejo*; of a language that, emerging from a Latin source, branches off in many respects from the Spanish spoken on the Iberian Peninsula; and of the American visual arts, which achieved their most glorious heights in the great Quito School of the colonial period.[46] It is a new cuisine, unique to the Cauca River Valley for its significant Afro-descendant component, with strong ties to the cuisine of the Caribbean and of other Spanish American peoples where an African spirit simmered, over a low flame, along with traces of Andalusian, Moorish, pre-Hispanic, and Castilian cultures. It was, in its time, a new cuisine, a popular creation, responsible, here and in other parts of the continent, for what José Rafael Lovera called a "gastronomic Golden Age."[47]

Travelers in the nineteenth century refer to this cuisine as the art of "regional cooking" to indicate its singularity. It produced a smorgasbord in which were combined peanuts, green papaya, meats and fishes, chili peppers, coconut, rice, beans, spices, and hundreds of fruits and vegetables whose flavors and aromas we have forgotten. The arrival of modernity and the penchant among Latin American elites for imitating everything European—especially the French, in the case of cooking—have deprived us of this wealth, to which we must return, for this forgotten feast represents one of the most authentic aspects of our culture.

But this proposition, if left in the realm of the senses, has no force. Of course, there are those, where the senses and taste are concerned, who find sufficient justification for treating this aspect of our culture as something that goes beyond its region of origin and refers, truly, to vast areas of Latin American culture. But that would be an exception to the rule and would run the risk of trivializing the theme or converting it into a mere question of recipes or culinary techniques. One must look to another level to find—beneath the charm of these gastronomic preparations—social relations, codes of communication, symbolism, and a complex fabric that underlies the peculiar formation of Creole communities.

The neoclassicist Andrés Bello, in a suggestive article titled "Las repúblicas hispanoamericanas: Autonomía cultural" (The Spanish American republics: Cultural autonomy), advanced the concept of continental unity in affirming that a "considerable number of nations situated on a vast continent and identical in institutions and origin . . . , customs and religion, will form over time a respectable *corpus*, one that counterbalances European politics." And at that very point he signals the need to "know in depth the nature and needs of the people . . . , listen with attention and impartiality to the voice of experience," and dedicate oneself "to observation" in order "to discover the inclinations, customs, and character" of the societies that constitute the apparently heterogeneous Latin American cultural universe. For Bello, understanding the cultural traits, the Latin American manner of being, that peculiar "nature," was prior to any processes of political unity or forms of governance.[48]

This essay, an inquiry into the alimentary habits of a region of Latin America, subscribes to that thesis. And since cooking, as an element of culture, at least where research is concerned, cannot rely on an elaborate specialized bibliography, it has been necessary to turn toward literature, particularly the great Latin American romantic novel *María*, a fruit of the same climes, in search of suggestions, indications, observations, and certainties that might permit us to unravel the hidden networks of culture through which we navigate. Although localized, these networks have a continental dimension that will help us to better understand our "inclinations, customs, and character."[49]

MARÍA

Close to a century and a half after its initial publication, *María*, Isaacs's singular novel, still engages readers.[1] For Seymour Menton, this miracle of literary survival is no coincidence. It is a matter of the magnum opus of American Romanticism, which "is maintained today by the clear artistic conscience with which Isaacs conceived and elaborated it."[2] Jorge Luis Borges asserted something similar in 1937, but he found the explanation of the novel's disquieting modernity, despite its dealing with a lost world, not so much in its romantic spirit as in its realism. For Borges, Isaacs is a man "who doesn't get along badly with reality," and neither did the style of the novel seem to him to be "excessively romantic." In fact, the Argentine writer praised the "Homeric joy of Isaacs in things material," as well as his "enthusiasm for everyday things."[3]

María, it is true, beyond its plot and the imaginary nature of its characters, can be read as a historical document, as a pleasant realistic chronicle on the society and culture of a Latin American region in the first half of the nineteenth century. That is the source of a good part of its currency and of the interest aroused by its reading. Its plot even provides an account of a social reality that indelibly marked the processes of formation of the family among the Latin American elites of the period. Efraín and María's frustrated idyll and its explanation—suggested masterfully through economic inequalities and patriarchal aspirations—is in the end a realistic fiction that portrays certain types of behavior and prejudices that can still be found in Latin American communities today.

As a realistic novel, *María* focuses on those elements of culture that form the nucleus of social relations, indicate membership in a certain ethnicity or class, and constitute symbols of identity. In specific, speaking and cooking acquire importance in and of themselves, for the routine of daily life in the novel's predominant atmosphere of isolation turns speech and cuisine into key moments in the relations between characters. The exceptional is hunting a jaguar, the death of and

FIG. 9 *Interior of a Dining Room in Santa Marta,* 1836

mourning over a former slave, a wedding celebration, and a prolonged trip to the metropolis—at that time London.

The sociolinguistic aspects of the novel are yet to be analyzed: the use of the *voseo* (the very familiar form of "you") and of diminutives, the differences between spoken and written language, the remnants of Castilian archaisms, the presence of Quechua and Africanisms, the realistic dialogues, the song lyrics, the overall narrative structure, and so on—and the relation of all the preceding to the customs and culture of the era. These make for attractive and varied material to help us better understand Latin American societies in the period just after the Wars of Independence and, consequently, understand the most profound distinguishing features of being Latin American today.

Here we limit ourselves to dealing with alimentary habits, for the linguistic themes exceed our competence. Cooking as a cultural product can be found page after page in *María*. It is possible that it is there for reasons of local color, more as a description than as an artistic delving into the question of taste, entailing combinations of flavors, colors, and aromas; it is this human sense that Isaacs explores least. Nonetheless, his multiple references constitute a guide that is as realistic as the rest of the novel. From that phenomenon emerges a cultural universe that strikes us as both remote and close, because Colombia's modernity did not imply a radical rupture from the past, and the formation of its urban communities has been produced not so much by the industrialization of the countryside as by the *ruralization* of the city.[4] That is one of the paradoxes of Latin America.

Cooking and the Division of Labor

Since those people are coming tomorrow, the girls are very
anxious to have some fine dishes ready.

—Isaacs, *María*, 40

Very well said. The truth is that María, the heroine of the novel, does not cook. Neither do the other young ladies of the patriarchal estate cook, nor the Latin American ladies who govern the ancestral homes. For this reason they are not *preparing* the desserts, but they are *very anxious* that they turn out perfectly. It is a matter of complex elaborations, for one must labor for two days. With this indication Isaacs reveals to us, in a single phrase, both the place the diverse social sectors occupy in the daily activities of the house and the arduous work the traditional cuisine requires.

Those desserts would be prepared by the black slaves, the true stewards of the kitchen, within which the master-slave relationship was the linchpin of the economic system. This is the primary characteristic of the Cauca Valley estate that forms the setting for *María*. From Isaacs himself we will learn that those sweets may be custard or fruit jelly, and from his contemporaries, like Luciano Rivera y Garrido or the North American traveler Holton, dulce de leche or the sweetened citrus compote called *desamargado*.

None of these are simple to prepare, even in season. And at least two are still difficult today, although now they can be bought ready-made in conventional groceries or supermarkets. We can assume that it was not a matter of custard or jelly, for those desserts were the most common and were, as Isaacs tells it, served customarily by the peasants of the region as part of the daily menu. Since it was a special occasion—the gentlemen came from the nation's capital, and one of them, Efraín's friend, with the intention of asking for María's hand—the sweets too ought to be singular, a token of esteem, something worthy of a notable visit. Dulce de leche, doubtless, with its Asian reminiscences and the time required to prepare it (overnight), must have been the dessert that had the maids all atwitter—not the citrus compote, since it is traditionally a Christmas dish and requires several days to be prepared correctly.

This dulce de leche is taken to be a typical dish of the Cauca Valley. The fact that the ingredients are cow's milk, sugar, and rice would appear to confirm that assertion. During the period when *María* takes place, the Cauca River Valley was a zone of extensive dairy herding and sugarcane plantations, as well as rice paddies sown in the flooded islets. The estate of El Paraíso (Paradise), where the novel unfolds, is a setting that, according to the protagonist Efraín, "my father had improved . . . [with] a costly and beautiful sugar refinery, many acres of sugarcane to supply it, extensive meadows with cattle and horses, good feeders."[5] Meat, milk, sugar, and rice—all were in the environs. And this will apply to most estates in the Cauca Valley, although few can boast a modern sugar refinery. Dulce de leche, to be sure, must be the dessert that corresponds to this type of economy.

Cooking it requires time, patience, physical strength, and the magical quality known as "feel." This quality permits the expert cook to know the precise quantities of the ingredients and their respective cooking points without measuring doses and without a cookbook. It was done, and it is still done, by cooking, in great copper pots, fresh milk with sugar and a good measure of rice soaked and ground into flour, which serves to thicken the sweet mixture. It is cooked over a wood fire, at a high temperature, for a long period of time. Forty liters of milk, which is the norm, require almost six hours of labor. And it should be stirred constantly with a *cagüinga*, a long wooden spoon, until it is just right. This task is called "beating the dulce de leche."

It was a task for strong slaves, those who could tolerate heat and prolonged effort. Sometimes, out of prejudice, it was considered a job for one lone female slave, for it was thought—it is still thought—that certain humors could curdle the sweet ingredients and ruin the delicate undertaking. The family gathers round; the young ladies, who can't endure fifteen minutes stirring the thick mixture—the more it is reduced, the harder it is to stir—urge the slaves on; the children play nearby while they wait their turn to scrape the kettle once the cooking is done; and the air fills with syrupy aromas that whet the appetite. Once it is ready it is poured into vessels made from the gourds of the *totumo* tree. It can be eaten warm, after a short while, but it is better at room temperature, the following day—better still, several days later, when the air and the warmth cause their surface to evaporate and form a hazel nut–like skin, which keeps the inside creamy, shiny, and exquisite. As it is made of milk, it goes very well with a glass of cold milk or over a thick slice of fresh cheese. It will be a tasty delight for the gentlemen who "are coming tomorrow."

The merriment of preparing the dulce de leche overshadows the division of labor. It is the lot of some to cheer on, others to cook. The ladies and gentlemen expect to be attended to; the slaves bring firewood for the fire and, of course, have already milked the cows at dawn, separated the calves, led the livestock to pasture, mended the fences, cultivated the earth by hand or pickax, or spent intense hours in the hell of the sugar mill, among other tasks. Nonetheless, beating the dulce de leche is a special event that brings together master

FIG. 10 Sirouy, *Dancing the Bambuco in the Village of El Bordo*, 1875–76

and laborers. Some swig distilled brandy for the occasion, and even the one who beats the sweet mixture sings. When dusk falls, when the dish is almost ready, and the slaves have finished their day's labor, a drum might appear, or perhaps a flute or some *guasás*.[6] There may be a *bambuco* or perhaps another dance. A sensitive child, as was Isaacs, would later remember, with nostalgia, that apparent joy when masters and slaves coexisted on the patriarchal estate.

Something very similar happened around other hearths during North American slavery, where the Afro-Americans created a Creole cuisine, borrowing from everywhere and contributing their own share. Doris Witt, in her *Black Hunger*, tells us of the old mammies of the US South, who arose at dawn to prepare, several hours later, the traditional beaten biscuits, which adorned their masters' table and delighted the children. Craig Claiborne, one of those children, also remembers that with nostalgia, and he tells us that his mother, "a southern belle among belles, adored beaten biscuits and often served them when she received her guests for afternoon coffee or tea."[7]

Preparing these biscuits from the Mississippi Delta, a creation and concoction of so many "Aunt Jemimas," whether their forebears could be traced back to Hispanic or French cuisines or not, was among the hardest chores in the realm of the southern kitchen. Made from a mixture of wheat flour with butter, cold water, and sometimes a bit of milk, the dough is beaten against a solid surface incessantly for nearly an hour, until it becomes elastic, smooth, and full of bubbles gathered from the surrounding air. Then it is stretched and cut into circles that are baked until they are crunchy, without becoming overly browned. Claiborne could hear, from his nursery at dawn, the constant whack upon whack upon whack produced by the biscuit dough as it was beaten.

Beating dulce de leche, or biscuits, whether in a tropical Latin American valley or on a plantation of the United States' Deep South, was therefore a task reserved for the black servants. A hard job that remained beyond the duties of the family's ladies or lasses, but by constituting an essential element of the culture, it came to undergird the customs and traditions of the landed class. The old mammies, analogous to the black women cooks of the Cauca Valley, marked profoundly—with their cooking, their speaking, and their music—the ladies and gentlemen of the southern plantations. Claiborne confesses that he had a black nanny, whom he called Aunt Catalina, who was, in fact, his proxy mother. In Isaacs's novel we learn that Nay, the old African princess, was like a mother to María. Later a poet situated to the south of the territory that Isaacs inhabited would tell us, "My nanny was black and like stars of silver / her eyes shone moist in the shadow." Overwhelmed with nostalgia, he would ask, "Why don't you rock me any longer, oh, my amorous night, / in the valley of tepid herbs of your lap?"[8]

When he wrote *María*, Isaacs was aware that the idyllic nature of master-slave relations on the estates of his homeland was a mere illusion. In an article published in the newspaper *La República* of Bogotá, on July 10, 1867, when the novel was already finished, he wrote that "slavery was an iniquity."[9] But in the novel the iniquities are nowhere to be found. Quite the contrary, the slaves are, one supposes, cheerful, they behave obediently, and the relations between them and their lords appear to be devoid of all tension. One could even think that they achieve a certain degree of fraternity. Why this abysmal difference between his expressed personal convictions and the picture he paints in his fiction?

One good explanation is nostalgia. The memories of infancy—with its aromas of meadows, flavors of fruits and candies, warmth and tenderness of the black nannies, friendship of the domestic slave who accompanied him in games and fishing and hunting trips—are the novel's raw material. It is also a fact that the primitive conditions under which the slaves labored did not extend to the family home. The adult who remembers his childhood does not sense it under the shadow of the master's whip. Those iniquities did not form part of his memory. There is awareness of the sweet flavor of the dulce de leche and the games played around the heavy pot, but not of the hardships necessary to make those things possible.[10]

It is even possible that Isaacs is right, and that the slave regimen of the specific universe of his father's estate was attenuated by good treatment, by the paternalism of the relations between masters, slaves, sharecroppers, and tenants. Peter Kolchin, in *American Slavery* (1993), warns us against unilateralism in analyzing the institution of slavery and draws our attention to the diversity of its manifestations. He documents the differences that existed in the situation of the different groups of slaves according to their crafts, the type of economy in which

FIG. 11
Brazilian Slaves, 1852

they were situated, the region they inhabited, the climate, and, of course, the disposition and temperament of the master they served. For Kolchin that diversity has contributed to numerous differences among historians on the meaning of slavery, in the sense that for every assertion in one direction one can find an example of its opposite.

In fact, Gilberto Freyre terms it a "softened" institution for a good part of Brazil, and Germán Colmenares, in studying the case of the government of Popayán—the region where the novel *María* is set—finds a laid-back, freer environment, with lenient controls, where the slaves of the livestock ranches lived or the sugar-mill estates of the Cauca River Valley stood.[11] That might explain the merriment of the dulce de leche preparation scene. It would be a gift for the landowners but also an occasion for trading, for singing, for consolidating social relations. It correlates to a less stringent institution, for it is a cultural product of which the Afro-descendants have taken ownership. It would become the symbol of "Cauca Country," as Isaacs called his native region, because it constituted a culinary allegory of the regional economy and because it represented, in its elaboration, the effort of most of the people who settled the area.

This effort and its corresponding social division of labor, in which some carry out chores that are demanding and others enjoy the fruits of those labors, also help us understand that, despite appearances, even under conditions of good treatment, slavery is still an "iniquity." Isaacs also shows this in his novel, when he introduces us to the world of Emigdio, the son of an owner of a medium-size property who lives near Efraín's paternal estate. In a dialogue that is memorable for what it suggests, Efraín asks him, "What have you been doing?" and receives the following reply, "We are butchering today, and as my father went off early, I have been directing the darkies—and it's a job," with which we begin to realize that slavery extended to other social sectors and was not the exclusive privilege of the large landowners. We also see that the slaves' food was rationed and that, within the mentality of the young master, taking care of that was a bother or nuisance. Right after that we are told that, upon hearing Emigdio's shout, "a half-naked negro boy appeared; one of his arms was shriveled and covered with scars." Efraín asks Emigdio, "How did that boy hurt his arm so badly?" And Emigdio answers, "Putting cane in the mill. Such stupids, they are! All he can do now is to mind horses."[12] Efraín makes no comment whatsoever on these affirmations, in which both the brutal character of the master-slave relation and the indifference of the masters toward the suffering of the slaves are revealed. The brutality is even more significant in this case, for an observation about the frizzy hair, albeit light colored, of the young servant, suggests that the poor boy might well be a half brother of the master who treats him with such scorn.

These iniquities occurred in Isaacs's world. The anthropologist Luis Francisco López Cano, in an important exploration that combines bibliographic research, fieldwork, archival documentation, and oral-history gathering, uncovers a good part of the reality underlying the universe of *María*, from which the following testimony emerges:

Our farm was surrounded by those of La Providencia, La Dolores, and La Margarita. La Margarita belonged to Don Pedro Vicente Gil; La Dolores to Don Rafael Gómez; and La Providencia to Don Modesto Cabal Galindo, the Elder, the first owner of Providencia. Providencia later belonged to the Polanco woman. She sold it to Cabal. She showed such bad faith with her slaves! . . . My father happened to witness all this. They cooked sugar syrup and emptied it into large vats made from broad tree trunks. In those days they knew nothing of metal containers: clay pots, gourd ladles, that's what they served us with. . . . What happened was that one of her (the Polanco woman's) slaves was frying something, and she burned what she was frying. Her mistress called two slaves to grab her by the arm and give her a whipping, leaving the poor thing naked. It was a Sunday, the day they gave her this beating. At midnight they began to grind the sugarcane, and the mill workers left the vats from the day before. That night, after the whipping, the slave woman got drunk and fell asleep in one of the vats. They arrived at three in the morning and were emptying the boiling syrup when they saw something leaping around inside the vat! . . . Well, it was the black woman, on fire! She was burning, the black woman was! The Polanco woman had a graveyard there, to bury the slaves.[13]

Even if this reality is not harshly revealed in the novel, it was part of Isaacs's world, in the locale of the estate where he spent his infancy. It was not made explicit for the simple reason that the narrative point of view of the literary text is that of Efraín, a young patrician, and not of Isaacs. But the author suggests it masterfully, and it's up to the competent reader to decipher it. We should know that the slave who beats the dessert does so under duress and that she could not fail at her task. The threat, always present, of punishment, which could have terrible consequences, lay hidden behind the sweetness of the dulce de leche and festive atmosphere that surrounded its preparation.

This dulce de leche, although long known in Spanish Andalusia and initially composed of ingredients brought by the Spaniards, would acquire Creole credentials of citizenship and would be perfected by the local cooks in a long process of exchanges whose roots lie deep in the colonial period.[14] The process is an integral part of the experience of the descendants of slaves in the Americas. With raw materials unknown in the lands they came from, they would show their adaptive capacity to the American tropics and would appropriate ideas that were either Hispanic or from elsewhere in Europe to create a new culture, one in which cooking would be an essential element. And not only in the tropics: Witt cites a letter in which a black woman shares with her daughter a recipe for turkey gravy, which contains "chili peppers, corn bread, and peanut butter, which I sense is African."[15] Although none of the components of the gravy are African, and certainly not the turkey, it is very possible that the old cook is right in a certain sense, for the adaptation of this concoction constitutes a part of the Afro-descendants' experience in America. Where dulce de leche is concerned, as it was prepared in Isaacs's time— and as it is still concocted when it is done right—this assertion is surely valid.

Sweets and Sexuality

During the meal I had the chance to admire, among other
things, the ability of Salomé and my godmother to roast
half-ripe plantains and cheese curds, fry fritters, prepare
pandebono, and temper the jelly.

—Isaacs, *María*, 155

That was how things really were, except that Efraín focused his admiration on *other things*, something that happened to him every time he dealt with matters of the kitchen and cooking. A subtle link between cooking and sensuality is established in Isaacs's novel, and the mild-mannered protagonist is besieged by furies beyond his control. Recently arrived from Bogotá, seated at the table of the family home at dinnertime, he finds several of his appetites are awakened at once. The utterance "María kept her eyes hidden from me resolutely; yet I could see that they had the brilliance and beauty belonging to those of the women of her race, in the instant when, despite herself, she let them fall full upon me" indicates a certain timidity that he will soon abandon. Later he speaks of her "moist, red lips," which suddenly will open to reveal the "beautiful arc of her teeth." Stupefied with María's presence at the table, he tells us, "I admired her beautifully turned arms and her hands as delicate as a queen's."[16]

The same kind of thing happens to him later, when, at the nearby house of a peon, he is served a *tortilla* soup that causes in him a certain impulse, for he confesses to us mischievously, "While we were eating, I caught a glimpse of one of the girls peeking through a half-opened door, and her pleasant face, lighted up by great black eyes, made me think that what was hidden ought to harmonize well with what could be seen."[17] Something similar happened to Master Giacomo Casanova with a Mexican brunette in Lisbon, which almost led to his death. She prepared for him some sweet *tortillas* made of walnuts, which he consumed while she looked at him with "unfathomable black eyes," according to his memoirs.[18] Giacomo, we know, also enjoyed *what was hidden*, whereas Efraín scarcely did so, even in his imagination.

Another servant girl, a vivacious daughter of the forest, knowledgeable perhaps of the old precept of Juan Ruiz (the medieval Spanish archpriest of Hita)—which equates "providing sustenance" with "carnally knowing an attractive female"—serves him a "succulent" lunch with beans, creamed corn, and *gamuza* (chocolate with corn flour and unrefined sugar) and equips him for the jaguar hunt with a meal that contains corn dough, fresh cheese, roast beef, and pieces of brown sugar. Later Efraín tells us that "Lucía came up to ask me about my rifle, and, as I was showing it to her, she added, in a low voice, 'There was no accident, was there?' 'None whatsoever,' I answered, affectionately *tapping her lips with a twig*."[19] The entire scene is charged with mischief, and we learn later, when everyone else goes back to work, that Lucía prepares a mattress of ponchos for his siesta, in a hidden place lulled by the "sounds of the river." That's all we know, but we can infer much more.

The idea of the relation between cooking and sexuality is so powerful in the Latin American imaginary that even Isaacs's chaste novel varies its tone, and even the naïf Efraín turns into a seasoned rogue when the text puts the servant girls in contact with the young gentlemen. Salomé, a fleshy young mulatto

FIG. 12
A. de Neuville, *Baking
Corn Bread*, 1869

woman from the Cauca Valley meadows, a tropical counterpart of the highland girl, or the Moorish girl, in the archpriest of Hita's *Book of Good Love*, awakens his instincts and stimulates his senses, especially that of taste, when she grills for him *pintones*, cheese curds, and fried dough; browns *pandebonos*; and regales him with jelly. Efraín loses his composure and tells us of her "teeth of an unreal whiteness, inseparable companions of moist and amorous lips," "her naked and delicate arms," "her unbound hair that rustled on her shoulders," and her "haunches," and he raves about "that waist and saunter, and that bosom, which seemed, rather than real, imagined."[20]

Salomé is the representation of the mixed-blood Cauca Valley woman, a descendant of slaves and an inhabitant of the fertile valley of the River Cauca, heir of the cultural traditions of the members of the common people in Spanish colonial times and repository of the culinary wisdom achieved over three centuries of isolation and transculturation. She is, besides, a sexual fetish for any young man of the upper classes and, especially, for Efraín, the oldest son of the local landowner. At the time the institution known as *droits de seigneur* (literally "lord's rights," with specific reference to privileged access to the virginity of

newlywed servant women) still existed. This practice was not only in the imagination but an actual prolongation of feudal privileges that reigned in Spanish
America. It was reinforced, furthermore, when combined with the regime of slavery. Young mulatto women, sculpted in the fire of hard physical labor—"nymphs
of the plains," as Holton called them in his visit through the Cauca Valley—are
an irresistible temptation for any master and even for *amitos* (young masters)
like Efraín.

The women knew it and, freer with their sexuality than the repressed white
women of the elite, they used it for the benefit of their descendants and their
families. This explains the prejudices on display, even among the less ignorant
of the upper-class male Creoles. Attracted by these women rife with vitality, the
men exercised a sexual dominance that emanated from both slavery and feudal-
ism, but they would write terribly about the Afro-descendant women. There were
exceptions, of course, and more than a few masters would marry their female
slaves and form legitimate families with them or civil unions that became permanent. That, along with sexual possession—consensual or otherwise—is where
the mulatto race comes from. That is where Salomé comes from. But there will
always be the stigma of texts like that of the influential Francisco José de Caldas,
called "the Wise," who refers to black men as "brutally lascivious, who engage
unreservedly in the sale of women. And the women, perhaps even more licen-
tious, serve as harlots without blushing and without remorse."[21]

The braid wound by weaving the strands of cooking, women, and sexuality
is ancient and constitutes a myth of the species. And slavery would reinforce it
in various parts of the world. In our case the black or mulatto woman as both
mistress of the kitchen and sex symbol would be a common image that we share
with the South of the United States, Caribbean plantations, Afro-Portuguese
Brazil, and the rest of the regions of America where the mixing of blood figured
as a dominant process in the construction of a Creole identity. An Asian impulse,
an Arabic vein that sailed in the slave ships and could be found in the conduct
of both Andalusian sailors and sub-Saharan slaves, would lend nuances to this
myth and help explain different behavior patterns.

Salomé, let us remember, sweetens Efraín with sugar and fruits, in this case
tropical fruits, guavas or blackberries, a combination that Creolizes them. And
perhaps the doughnuts were bathed in syrup. The mulatto woman thus prepares,
without knowing it, the same Mozárabe (Christian-Moorish) mixture that orig-
inated in the Muslim world and that the caliphate of Córdoba enthroned in the
cultural universe of the European peninsula. Dulce de leche, custard, doughnuts,
cheese crullers, citrus compote, jellies, syrups, and puff pastry are all delicacies of North African cooking that Salomé prepares, with a touch proper to the
Cauca Valley, in an alchemy that will engender the regional cuisine of this part
of the tropics, replacing one ingredient with another, adjusting the points of

perfection, and measuring the ingredients of each preparation, for that is what the habitat and ethnic mixture require. The names would vary—*almojábana* would become pandebono (both words for cheese cruller) and *letuario* would be called *desamargado* (both terms for sweetened citrus compote)—and the taste would be slightly different, not only because of the new ingredients, especially the corn, but also because things taste different in different climates. Despite everything, the Asian traces would not be lost, and, in a singular way, the imagery associated with each of these combinations would persist.

One of those ideas, as persistent as any, connects foods that are sweetened with sugar, or with cane syrup, to sexuality. Claude Lévi-Strauss, Xavier Domingo reminds us, documents a great number of myths that grant erotic powers to foods cooked with honey. The Arab people, in turn, introduced to medieval Hispania the suggestion of the relation between sex and sweets. Domingo references a curious text titled *Speculum al joder* (Speculum on screwing), which was a translation into the Valencian language (a dialect of Catalan), done between the fourteenth and fifteenth centuries, of an ancient Arabic manuscript in which that link is extended to almost every aspect of cooking.[22]

Long before Salomé, in Juan Ruiz's *Libro de buen amor* (Book of good love), deep within the period of medieval Arabic Spain, a beautiful girl, desirous of "doing battle" with Don Melón de la Huerta (Sir melon of the garden), serves him abundant butter, grilled cheese, milk, and custard. And the Go-Between, or Matchmaker, who is all-knowing, teaches that "he who loves not nuns is worth not a whit," for the latter are experts in many delicacies, many "citrus compotes, noble and so strange." They make the best lovers, for "all the sugar resides within them: rolled up, powdered, lumped, and candied, and very pink; crystallized sugar and beaten sugar, and many other preparations I can't begin to recall."[23]

Our citrus compote is a lecherous meal. In the baroque picaresque novel *La vida del buscón* (Life of the rogue), Quevedo y Villegas characterizes it as a sweet with which the "wily women" would regale the men on the street, along with a shot of brandy, to whet their dormant appetites. Domingo borrows from the book by Diego Granado, *Libro del arte de cocinar* (Book of the art of cooking), published in the seventeenth century, a recipe that warrants being known by all:

> Cut the skin of an orange into four quarters and soak the skins in water for ten days; cook them when the water is well cured, lightening their color, and, when they become translucent or transparent, they are done. Then remove them with two clean dishrags and rinse them very well and put them into a pan or pot or cauldron and pour over them such a quantity of sugar syrup that they are more than half covered. Boil, stirring constantly, and remove them quickly from the fire so that the syrup does not harden or overcook. Afterward let them sit for four days. Each day you must stir

them three times. Then take them out and drain the syrup and put them to cook again in an appropriate amount of syrup. After they have cooked for the length of time it takes to recite one credo, remove them from the fire and pour them into containers.[24]

Domingo clarifies that if the orange was extracted and the juice set aside, this formed a sort of jam, compote, or sugar syrup. Among us this compote evolved into *desamargado* and became a fine crystallized candy, customary to give as a Christmas gift. Women like Salomé would cook it to perfection. Let us look at our recipe, sweetened lime compote, proper to Cauca Valley cuisine, such as was published in the book *Platos de las abuelas* (Dishes of our grandmothers):

Take three limes, rub them one by one against a rough tile or grindstone, cut them in half and with a small spoon extract all the flesh, inserting the spoon between the peel and the rind so that all the pulp comes out, and then place them in water over a fire. . . . Once they are cooked, diminish their bitterness by soaking them in water for three or four days. Make syrup with a pound and a half of sugar per dozen whole limes, and, when they are cool and well drained, mix the limes into the syrup and let them simmer over a low flame. When they are translucent, but before the syrup thickens, remove them from the heat, let them rest a while, and then add a spoonful of rum (if desired) and serve.[25]

The ancient tradition of the "wily women" would most likely wish to include the shot of rum so that the reduction would incite young men to audacities that might lead to "doing battle." We do not know if the jam with which Salomé regaled Efraín was derived from the liquid of some compote (for although those of orange and lime—fruits proper to the Arabs—were more common, it could be made from any fruit, as *The Book of Good Love* tells us), but all the same it induced the affected young gentleman to engage in unusual behavior. Efraín grew delirious over the mulatto woman's scent "of mallows," and he ended up bathing nude in the river, while the provocative Salomé, hidden around some nearby bend, floated flower petals down with the current, letting him know of her disquieting proximity.[26]

This cuisine, which combines the sweetness of sugar, the saltiness of cheese curds, and the bittersweetness of semiripe plantains, is redolent with suggestiveness. It is not Arabic, not Hispanic, not African, and not indigenous—no matter how replete it may be with allusions to these cultures—but a new creation, for at its foundations lies American slavery. We must never lose sight of the fact that *María* is a novel set within a regime of slavery. This reality supposed a dramatic change for those who were slaves. As Sydney Mintz has demonstrated, black slaves had to recreate their most basic life patterns under new conditions, in strange habitats and without the institutional structure of their former societies.[27] Because of the central role of food, the creation of a cuisine under these new conditions formed a major, fundamental part of Cauca Valley culture. The origin of the raw materials is the least significant aspect of this process of cultural construction—although it does also count, as we shall see later.

Salomé's cooking draws the world together. There is the plantain, an immigrant from Asia and Africa; American corn, which will replace wheat in doughnuts; cow's milk from Europe; Arabian sugar; fruits from the South American tropics; and spices from all over. This variety of strange ingredients with which the new cuisine had to be created, plus the diverse cooking techniques and differing tastes among slaves and masters, tells us that the Afro-descendants in our territory had to reinvent a cuisine under conditions more dramatically different than those of any other population in modern times. This is an experience common to all slaves in America.

That is why universal myths linking sugar and sexuality are an integral part of this experience. "The honey of your lips" is sung in Latin American boleros; North American men call their sweethearts "Honey"; Brazilian men call the one they desire "Sugar Baby"; and so on. Salomé, in accordance with that cultural compulsion, attends to the young gentleman with a suggestive dish, as did the mountain woman to Lord Melon or as would Pepita Jiménez to a disoriented candidate for the seminary in a lost Andalusian village around *María*'s time (1874).[28] The manner of cooking, although similar the one to the other, is distinct; the intentions of the young women, identical; the results: successful, about two-thirds of the time.

Cooking, Geography, and Region

"What a cunning flatterer she is!" said José. "Ah, Luisa," he
added, "there's good judgment for you! We don't understand
such things."
—Isaacs, *María*, 44

I know what you want—to run down to the ravine ahead of me
and then say that all the blackfish are on your hooks.
                                            —Isaacs, *María*, 62

The boatmen, with their trousers now on, gossiped with Rufina.
Lorenzo brought in some of his provisions to go with the stew
which Bibiano's daughter was making ready for us.
                                            —Isaacs, *María*, 178

The cooking of Salomé, Luisa, or Rufina (Bibiano's daughter) is more than just a compendium of products. As Roland Barthes has taught us, it is, at one and the same time, a reference to the natural conditions, a thread of traditions transmitted from one generation to the next, a system of communication between human beings, a code of social stratification, and a body of images, situations, and behaviors. In a word, as has been so often said and so seldom understood, cooking constitutes, alongside language, one of the two keys to human culture.[29] When Isaacs wrote his novel, he was a member of a new culture, formed in the Spanish colonial period, clearly manifested in cooking by the eighteenth century. The territory of this cooking, denominated "Cauca Country," goes beyond the boundaries of what is geographically known as the Cauca River Valley.

When we use that expression, we are referring not only to the elevated tropical plateau—on average, 1,000 meters (approximately 3,200 feet) above sea level—but also to the Pacific coast, separated from the plateau by the tall mountains to the west of the hacienda El Paraíso, the novel's setting (see map). The level areas are connected to one another by a series of roads, paths, and cuts, along which goods, animals, and human beings constantly move. The mountains, rough and scarred with deeps canyons, but also featuring small and peaceful valleys and rivers that are short in length but high in water volume, have since time immemorial functioned, rather than as an insurmountable barrier, as a bridge between the two plains.

Since the onset of the Spanish Conquest, the seaboard has drawn inhabitants to the high plateau. Gold was the first motivation, and foreign trade was the second. Countless caravans have moved in both directions on the paths connecting one plain to the other, forging a network of landmarks, inns, villages, and cities that formed a web of social relations that explains the cultural unity one finds between the populations of both regions. This constant coming and going is what allows us to speak of a greater Cauca Valley that surpasses the limits imposed by geography, beyond the banks of the river and encompassing marshlands, mangrove swamps, and the banks and mouths of tidal rivers. This traffic, especially where the slave trade was concerned, is responsible for constructing the cultural region that Isaacs calls "Cauca Country."[30]

As occurs with life on all levels of terrain, but especially on tropical plains, the constant presence of water and heat allows vegetable and animal existence to proliferate. Paradoxically, the ease with which one finds food is inseparable from the abundance of insects, bacteria, fungi, viruses, and all life forms that makes the territory unhealthy for human beings. This ease explains why the population continues to be slight, dispersed over vast spaces, and dependent on the mercy of the elements. Malaria, yaws, and respiratory and other illnesses become endemic, and deadly epidemics break out time and again. Often the population shrinks rather than grows. Richard Preston illustrates the situation

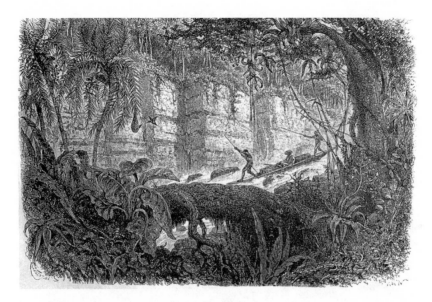

FIG. 13 A. de Neuville, *Navigating the Dagua River*, 1869

with the following example: "Smallpox epidemics ravaged the Valley in 1841 and again in 1871. In the latter year more than one thousand people died in the municipality of Cali alone. They piled up so many corpses in the public cemetery that the gravedigger complained that he would have to exhume cadavers to inter others that were being brought every day."[31]

Buenaventura, one of the axes of Cauca Country, suffered even more than Cali from these conditions, as did all the Pacific lowland, for there the heat and humidity are even more extreme. As a result, the low marshlands were avoided as a site of permanent settlement by both the Spanish and the Creole elite and were left as territory to be populated by indigenous communities that had survived the Spanish Conquest and by large groups of slaves and their descendants. The masters would suffer the hardships of the interior plain, but they would not subject themselves to the scorching and floods of the coastal lowlands. Here is how Gaspard Mollien describes Buenaventura in 1823:

> For the strategic importance and beauty of its location, Buenaventura ought to be a major city; its port ought to host active trade; a rich and industrial population ought to fill its streets; and numerous boats ought to come and go incessantly, but there is nothing of the sort. [There are] a dozen huts inhabited by blacks and mulattos, a military barracks with a guard of eleven soldiers, three pieces of artillery. The governor's house, as well as that of

FIG. 14 Niederhausern-Koechlin, *Port and Roadstead of Buenaventura*, 1869

customs, is constructed of straw and bamboo, situated on the islet of Cascajal, covered with grass, thorns, mud, snakes, and frogs: that is Buenaventura.[32]

That was the state of things. The most powerful landowners sought the mountain foothills, the higher ground, in constructing their dwellings, leaving the floodplains, wetlands, and swamps to the peasants, slaves, and freedmen to inhabit. This situation is reflected in Isaacs's novel: "Before sunset, I had seen my father's house *whitening on the shoulders of the mountains*," Efraín tells us at the start.[33] The climate there, although still sharing in the stresses proper to a tropical habitat, would be a bit more temperate. Along the Pacific coast one finds the same thing: the mining settlements were established in the foothills of the western mountain range, near the headwaters of the rivers, and from there the fugitive slaves or freedmen would fan out, heading downstream, to populate the river valleys surrounded by marshes and close to mangrove swamps.

In any case the houses were built near the rivers or wetlands. This was so partly because flood plains had become a way of life but also partly because of the river's functional value as a means of communication and transportation and as a source for food.[34] The villages of the inland plain and the lowland would have the character of river settlements, even though most of the inhabitants were shepherds, farmers, miners, and lumberjacks. Fishing was an activity common to all, but the exclusive trade of only a few.

In the preamble to this essay, I try to show the intimate relation between nutrition and fishing that forms the base for the traditional cuisine of the Cauca Valley. For Víctor Manuel Patiño, in his *Historia de la cultura material en la América equinoccial* (History of material culture in equatorial America), if one were to judge by the current situation, one would believe that the consumption of fish was scanty or nil in the inland plains and only customary in the maritime regions. This is a gross error, he tells us, and he adds, "The available documentation indicates that both on the coast and in the interior . . . fish consumption was intense and constant."[35] That is a fact, and this fact explains why Isaacs repeatedly mentions "fish" in the meals of *María*, as well as in the stews made of *nayo*. Fish was so common a foodstuff that, as we have shown, the Cauca Valley was known by the first Spanish chroniclers as the "province of the gorrones," alluding to an indigenous community whose name came from the abundant fish they caught and traded throughout the territory.[36] This gorrón was none other than the bocachico, a fish common to the rivers of South America, also found along the Pacific coast, near Chocó, where it is known as *chere*.

Isaacs dallies in the universe of the Pacific coast and shows us, among other things, its cuisine. As in the higher inland plains, he allows himself to be transported by the landscape, in this case that of a rain forest, and he tells us about the *naidí*, a palm tree from whose fruit one can make soft drinks, jellies, and preserves and whose bulb becomes the delicious heart of palm; about the *milpesos*, a good source of oil with a fruit that can be made into a hot drink that is beaten like chocolate; and about the *chontaduro*, a product of the *chonta* palm, which is a sort of panacea plant. From it one can derive a food of great nutritional value—which also is a staple of Cauca Valley cooking—and its wood can be used to construct houses, domestic utensils, and even the marimba, the most important musical instrument of these communities. From its bulb one can also derive the heart of palm, and its braided leaves can be used as bellows to fan fires.[37]

Fish was an everyday staple, just as on the inland plain, although along the Pacific, owing to the difficulty of raising cattle in the extreme climate, beef was scarce and would be procured by means of trade, in the form of jerked beef, brought as a ration that the masters would give to slaves in the mines or that would be sold at the weekly markets held on the riverbanks. "Cali meat stew" was the name given in Chocó to the cooked mixture of this salted beef with plantain and yucca, which was, just as on the inland plain, consumed by the common person.

The dedication to fishing entailed in life along the river would generate exceptions, however, when the chores of transporting on the rivers or catching fish extended over several workdays. Then, in contrast to the norm, the entire cooking process would become a man's job. That is what happens to Efraín when he is transported by a pair of oarsmen upriver from the Pacific, toward Cali: "That day's lunch was a duplicate of the previous one, except for an increase in the size of the dish that Gregorio had promised, a potage he prepared by digging a pit on the beach and lining it with *bijao* leaves, adding the meat, plantains, and the other ingredients that would make the stew, covering it with dirt and, on top of it all, lighting a fire."[38]

The result is a flavorful and juicy concoction, which in the upper valley would be called *sudado* (literally "sweated") and in other regions of the country *viudo* (literally "widower"), in which the ingredients simmer slowly in that kind of natural oven and the flavors of the tubers, fruits, vegetables, and condiments mix with the juices of the meats, in a mysterious subterranean alchemy that does not permit the loss of a single bit of juice that the foods exude. This form of cooking is ancient and has been documented in a variety of cultures. Felipe Fernández-Armesto tells us in his *Historia de la comida* (History of food) that "the cooking pit constituted an improvement of great importance in the history of cooking, in comparison to heated rocks. It took ingenuity to come up with this innovation. . . . Several experiments carried out in situ demonstrated that it was possible to roast large chunks of meat satisfactorily in just a few hours. . . . In clayish soil the inner lining of the pit would tend to turn into ceramic, which made the sides impermeable."[39] It was also a way to avoid knocking over the cookware, a feature that made the seminomadic work of the oarsmen easier.

Roast meat is still popular nowadays, although the custom of cooking in earth pits has largely been abandoned. Jaime Arocha, who for several days accompanied the fishermen of Tumaco, tells us that "the cook begins to prepare lunch. It is traditional to prepare *tapao*, which is cooked in an aluminum pot in which a layer of fish and little pieces of plantain are put and covered with banana leaves; then, a second layer of fish covered with *bijao* leaves, and so forth up to the brim. All you add is a little seawater, and you wait for the liquids of the leaves to lend it flavor."[40]

The result, although not quite identical, proves to be much like that produced by the older process. No matter the culinary technique, what stands out here, besides carrying on old traditions one generation after another, is the fact that we find ourselves within a male culinary domain, engendered by the tasks of fishing—or hunting, which is tantamount to the same—or by forms of life that are nonsedentary, as in the case of the oarsmen, who are engaged in a constant coming and going between different points along the river. But this would be the exception, just as it would be exceptional for some women to carry out the tasks of hunting and fishing. In general, just as in the whole universe of the kitchens in *María*, woman is, at one and the same time, master and slave of the kitchen.

By means of this relationship she would assume an essential role in community life and in the generation of culture. Even if, as happened in this case, she was also the slave of some concrete master and he should inhabit—which was unusual—the territories of the mines.

These women of the Pacific lowlands—mostly African American—would contribute three major concepts to regional cuisine: cooking with coconut, ceviche, and African fufú. All three were passed on to the women of the high plains and helped enrich popular taste. For Emilia Valencia, who writes from within this zone, "The base is constituted by all manner of fish and seafood, wildlife of the woods (deer, peccary, *guatín*, rabbit, etc.), plantain and corn, *all seasoned with the ever-present coconut water*."[41] Coconut itself, of course, would be eaten raw or grated, made into desserts or pastries, or used as the base for sweets or in soft drinks—lemonade prepared in coconut water is delightful—or fermented spirits. But most important is the combination of sweet and savory that comes from the use of coconut water in the cooking of various meats. That explains why, as we have seen, a representative of the British government in Popayán would be surprised, in the first half of the nineteenth century, when he was served as a main dish fish with fruit, which, according to him, he "had never seen before," and which seemed to him "exquisite victuals." A *pusandao* of fish—a dish that should be served in a broth—as it is prepared in Guapi, according to the version of Valencia, conveys the idea:

> You need fish, green plantains, yucca, *refrito*, clear coconut water, thick coconut milk, herbs (cilantro, unsweetened *yerba mate*, pennyroyal) and salt. Except for the fish, everything is set to cook in the coconut water until the plantain and the yucca are almost done, and then the fish and the coconut milk are added. Cover the pot and continue cooking over a low flame till the ingredients are sufficiently done and the fish, [is] cooked but still firm. It is served with a little finely chopped cilantro on top and accompanied by avocado and toasted plantain.[42]

The result is a culinary delight, even though, without a doubt, the fruity flavor of the coconut milk, with the avocado and the fried, smashed green plantain set to fry rapidly (which complements the *pusandao*), must have seemed a strange combination to a European palate at the beginning of the nineteenth century. The fruits are, to be sure, the coconut, avocado, plantain, and tomato that accompany the *refrito*. For the period none of these ingredients were typical in European cuisine.

Not only does coconut water produce a singular cuisine; it can also be used as a substitute for water in all types of recipes. In fact, that substitution characterizes the cooks in the lower climes, lending the cuisine its distinctive

FIG. 15 *Black People's Huts*, 1836

Afro-American flavor. Their counterparts in the interior valley, many of them involved in the trade between the two territories, would also find productive palm trees in the bottomland of the Cauca Valley and would add coconut to their recipes. Loaf brown sugar, or *cocada*, a sweet made of grated coconut cooked with brown sugar, would become a mainstay of peasant diets, as well as a favorite among children.

Culinary techniques also have their own history. This manner of cooking—making extensive use of coconut water—belongs to certain communities and alludes to traditions transmitted over centuries and territories separated by great expanses. It is common among other human groups from tropical Africa, Southeast Asia and India, and the Caribbean, both continental and insular. Knowing that the inhabitants of the Pacific lowlands are, for the most part, descendants of Africans, we may surmise that this culinary technique is a manifestation of a certain Africanness in the cultural universe of the Cauca River region, and the technique correlates to life forms, social deportment, and spiritual manifestations proper to the peculiar racial mixing predominant in this region of Latin America.

The same, however, cannot be said for ceviche. A delicacy, obtained by "cooking" raw meat of certain fish or shellfish in abundant lemon juice, sweet onions, sometimes tomatoes, aromatic herbs (generally cilantro), salt, and chili pepper, it is a common victual among people of the Pacific seaboard from the north of Chile to the Colombian port of Buenaventura. Chileans, Peruvians, and Ecuadorians engage in heated disputes over the "national character" of ceviche, or over its origin, without realizing that it is a *continental* dish, long known among the coastal village dwellers of all those areas. Within Colombia one does not hear well-informed voices participating in this polemic, perhaps because the Afro-descendant communities of the Pacific have a certain awareness that a good part of their traditions and customs "come from the South," alluding to the most ancient settlements, located in the mining territories of Barbacoas and Tumaco, much akin to present-day Esmeraldas Province in Ecuador.

The origins of ceviche remain murky. Some authors assume it has a pre-Hispanic origin, noting that the dish's distribution corresponds approximately to the limits of the old Inca Empire, although no documentation exists to prove this hypothesis. Others consider it a Creole hybrid, in which the Spanish, Creoles of the colonial period, and Afro-descendants participated, based on the combination of ingredients—Hispanic lemon and onions along with local foods—and its popularity as a dish among Afro-American communities. Still others, in brief, point to a possible Asian influence via the massive Japanese immigration to Peru in the latter part of the nineteenth century, granting it a source common to that of the culinary techniques of sushi and sashimi. Whatever the truth, it is nonetheless evident that ceviche exists across a broad stretch of South America and has a singular characteristic: because of its exact combination of ingredients, it is not like other dishes of raw meat found in other cultures. In the case of Colombia, there is no doubt that Afro-descendant cuisine is its cradle and the Cauca Valley its nursery. Here and elsewhere in Latin America, however, ceviche has grown to enjoy broad acceptance and general preference, thanks to its delicacy, slight acidity, exciting piquancy, and fresh flavor. Along with rice in coconut water, it is one of the two major contributions accorded by the kitchens of *María* to universal dining.

In contrast, there is no doubt whatsoever as to fufú. Isaacs mentions this in passing, in describing Rufina's house, on the banks of the Dagua River: "beyond the living room was a bedroom, which led to the kitchen, whose oven was formed by a great box of palm planks filled with earth, over which rested the stones and the apparatus for making the fufú."[43] He says this, nothing more, as if the reader of his era knew of this dish, or concoction, full well and therefore needed no further explanation. It was a matter of a common meal, nothing exotic, and familiar to all. To be honest, it was and still is so, although in our case the name has changed—even distancing itself considerably from the original, in some instances—and the preparation has undergone some modifications. Don Mario Carvajal, who read the novel a century after its initial appearance, believed it opportune to include a glossary at the end of the text, for some of the expressions had fallen into disuse, and others were regionalisms hard to understand outside the area of *María*'s setting. Of fufú we are told by Carvajal that it is a "dough made from green cooked plantain and substantial broth," with which we begin to understand better its origin and to imagine its taste.[44] The same dish today is called *bala* in Tumaco and green banana *mote* in the Colombian Caribbean. Only in Guapi will the similarity with the original word be maintained, calling it *jujú*, although in that Cauca Valley village the dough is prepared with ripe plantain.[45]

It belongs to the African culinary heritage, and it is one of the very few recipes that maintain the details of the cuisine of that vast and diverse continent. It is not a matter of Creole cuisine with a strong Afro-descendant component, as are almost all the recipes in *María*, but rather a concatenation of its own character and origin from different native communities of tropical Africa. An online page dedicated to African gastronomy tells us that "fufú, known by many other names, such as *pirao* or *funje* in Angola, *nsima* or *ugali* in the east . . . , serves as the dietary staple in many sub-Saharan countries. . . . It goes with all sorts of dressings and sauces. . . . To prepare it one can use all sorts of flour, according to the region. While in western Africa it is normal to use *ñame* alone or *ñame* with plantain, in central Africa yucca flour is more common, and in the east, corn flour."[46]

Phil Bartle, who lived with communities of the Akan peoples in Ghana, tells us that fufú is their most distinctive dish and that it was originally prepared with yam, even though today it is customary to mix plantain and yucca: "First you cook the yam (or the mixture of plantain and yucca). Then, in a mortar made from a hollow trunk, you prepare the dough."[47] It is served hot, without any dressing, and is used to soak up the soup or as a complement to different sauces and meats. According to his research, fufú in the Akan language means, literally, "white-white," so named for the characteristic color of the yam batter.

Fufú is found among various Latin American communities where the cultural influence of Afro-descendant populations is strong. In Cuba, for example, according to Guillermo Jiménez Soler, fufú is "a kind of boiled pickled plantain purée with meat or pork skin, garlic, and other condiments."[48] In the Dominican Republic it is called *mangú*, and in Puerto Rico it is known as *mofongo*, and it is made with fried mashed green plantain filled with pig cracklings. The same preparation is known in Cali as *marranita*, and it is extremely popular.

We are not dealing with just an African legacy in America. Rather, the descendants of slaves made variations in its preparation, enriched with new ingredients, from America back to Africa. Fernández-Armesto tells us, for example,

"Liberian *foo foo* is not elaborated from native millet but with the tapioca that the liberated slaves who founded the nation brought with them from the United States."[49] This idea of a soft pasta made of tubers (yam, yucca, *arum*, or Chinese potato); fruits (plantain, squash, or beans); or cereals (millet, corn, wheat, or rice) that goes with sauces, meats, and vegetables ranges from the couscous of the villages of the North African Magreb, passing through the *bolinhos* of Rio de Janeiro, extending to the *carimañolas* of the Caribbean, and spanning varieties that combine the savory with the sweet, like the *jujú* from Guapi or the *aborrajados* from the Cauca Valley.[50]

This history explains the ease with which Afro-descendant people assimilated the technique of fufú's pre-Hispanic counterpart—the tamale—whose preparation follows the same culinary principles. These cooks varied the envelope. In using banana leaves instead of corn, they prolonged the cooking until they found a better texture, and they even dared replace the ingredients of the dough by using green plantain, as happens with the *piangua* tamale of the Colombian Pacific; rice in the Chocóan and Caribbean pastries; or coconut water as a thinner and binder in the corn batter of the exquisite Guapi tamale. Fufú is a sort of gauge of the roots of Africanness in Latin American culture, roots that are revealed with special relevance in Cauca River Valley eating habits, as Isaacs makes manifest in his novel.

Food, Hunting, and Society

I found that the boys who, years before, had taught me to set
snares for the *chilacoas* and *guatines* in the thick woods were
now men.

—Isaacs, *María*, 8

José led me to the river and talked to me about his crops and
his hunting.

—Isaacs, *María*, 16

He probably means to go bear hunting. . . . It's really less
dangerous than deer hunting, and that's done everywhere and
all the while.

—Isaacs, *María*, 26

But eating and cooking also means acquiring food. Fishing is part of cooking just as planting seeds is. In fact, cooking begins with the act of finding raw materials. Of those kitchens in *María*, what are we told—beyond affirming the piscatory and amphibious wealth of the Cauca Valley habitat and revealing the cultural unity of the interior plains and the tidal zone—by the fact that *pejes, negros,* or *nayos* were dishes common to all tables? What does it mean beyond the specific manner of combining the ingredients?

One thing it tells us is that an important part of the region's diet came through hunting. Fishing is a form of hunting. In fact, even today, most fish harvests for human consumption are obtained by capturing wild animals in rivers, lakes, and seas rather than by fish farming. Although the same does not apply to land or air animals, in *María*'s times hunting still played an important role in supplying the daily food. Hunting was an everyday activity, a man's work, and part of his duty within the family matrix.

It is not the famous jaguar hunt—which is resolved with such solemnity in the novel—that is interesting as an index of the daily relationship between hunting, cooking, social organization, culinary practices, and the division of labor. It is of an exceptional nature and, in the case recounted in *María*, it serves more to illuminate the pastimes proper to the dominant groups. For the peasants as well as the slaves, hunting is a job, often a hard and dangerous task, often necessary to protect plantings and harvests, and, in most cases, a source of food and economic means. It signals a masculine space. Although there had to be women hunters—almost always young and dedicated to these activities during their free time—this would always be on an occasional, if not exceptional, basis. The hunt is essentially part of a man's universe. It would entail, repeatedly, a special effort, an additional chore requiring patience and vigor. The male world of the hunt should not be viewed as a space of pleasure, of recreation and camaraderie among companions—although it may permit that type of exchange, as may happen generally with all jobs—but as one of the most arduous aspects of Latin American life in the first half of the nineteenth century. Hunting as recreation—as we have already stated—is reserved for the powerful minorities. Idealizing the hunter as an icon of open spaces and a symbol of a free and carefree life stems from misunderstanding the difficulties and sacrifices that activity imposed.

During *María*'s time firearms were beyond the reach of the masses. They were articles of luxury for a few, and those arms that could be found in the possession of the peasants were hulking old things that often failed just when they were needed most. But the need to hunt was undeniable, not so much for nutritional needs as for reasons having to do with protecting the crops. The *nagüiblancas* (literally "white petticoats"), for example, constituted a plague that could ruin a whole planting by unearthing and eating the seeds. These enormous and ravenous pigeons would generally land in the groves of the foothills, quite a distance from the fields under cultivation. Reaching the birds required a long night's trek. Then, using torches and armed with slingshots, peering through the darkness, in silence, the hunters would proceed to knock down as

FIG. 16 Jean-Baptiste Debret, *Vendors of Milk and Straw*, 1835

many birds as possible. This was not done for pleasure but out of necessity. It was a hard job that could last into the wee hours of the night.

Back at home the women would wait, seated at long tables of coarse wood, engaged, one would hope, in excited and anticipatory prattle. When they sensed the proximity of the hunters, they would start the water boiling in large pots. Then they would pluck, open, gut, and clean the fowl, some of which they would fry immediately, without any dressing other than salt and chili, to satisfy their family's appetite for that evening. The rest was saved for the next day, salted and peppered, seasoned with lemon juice and vinegar, garlic and chopped cilantro roots. With that they would prepare *atollado* rice, using broth and the dark pigeon meat, with its special flavor. This *atollado* seems to be a derivative of fufú, but transformed, much as the African couscous, for instance, is made with yams instead of semolina. Our rice fufú, or *atollado* with doves—or with other meats—is a dish proper to the black villages of the Cauca Valley plateau.

If the hunting was abundant, a portion of the birds would be destined for the market. They would have to be preserved for a few days, something that would be accomplished by placing them, after they were dressed, in smokers located in the kitchen itself, on top of the wood cookstove. Wrapped in banana leaves, they would become part of the products the peasants and slaves brought to the village markets. They would enrich other tables, forming an essential part of economic life in a world that revolved around the institution of slavery.

Hunting could also be the key to local well-being. By adding new elements to the standard diet, the hunt would make market-day offerings more diversified. This variety in the slave—and later peasant—contribution to markets would also help explain the excitement, intermingling, and economic activity of the small settlements that arose at crossroads and river launch points. Market day would become an institution, not only commercially but also as an opportunity for community encounters, a space of cultural exchange, a break in the daily routine, a chance to establish new social relations, and a worksite for vendors and cooks, as well as a chance to be in touch with authorities and the world of politics. All this was made possible by food distribution, which is one of the primary and integral aspects of any cuisine.

The variety of these local markets can exceed one's expectations. And the fruits of the hunt can explain this phenomenon in good measure. The fishermen arrive with their catch, fresh or salted and dried; besides beef, pork, mutton, and domestic fowl, there is elk, capybaras (the world's largest rodent), venison, *iguasa* ducks, *nagüiblancas*, otter-like *guaguas*, turtles, and so on, not to mention cultivated products such as corn, rice, plantain, yucca, potato, vegetables, legumes, and others. There are also wild plants, among which are a great number of aromatic herbs and condiments, fruits of palm and exotic trees, or fruits and berries that grow in the wild.

An excellent example of these local markets in American slave territory is provided by Moreau de Saint Méry, writing about the market of Clugny in Santo Domingo, at the end of the eighteenth century, where fifteen thousand slaves congregated each Sunday to buy and sell their own wares.[51] It was the same at the Aguablanca Lagoon in Cali, toward the end of the colonial period, and even at the beginning of the twentieth century in the market of Juanchito in the same city—part of the setting of the novel *María*—where farmed and hunted products displayed on great reed rafts formed an extensive framework of vessels along the banks of the port on the Cauca River. Alejandro Sarasti Aparicio left a vivid description of this weekly event.[52]

The capture of each type of animal requires specialized techniques. If the quest is not for naguiblancas but for iguasas, a small duck with exquisite flavor that was of noteworthy abundance, the hunters would have to get up very early, with the dark that precedes the dawn, to place nets at the bottom of the pools of water, where these birds land at the first light of dawn; then they would wait hidden along the banks, enduring in silence the relentless stalking of the mosquitoes or, more dramatic, remaining still while a deadly poisonous snake slithers nearby through the hunters' lair. When the moment arrives, a swift upward movement of the net catches a significant number of iguasas by their feet and allows them to be snared by the hunting group. Steamed iguasa was so prized among Cauca Valley families that they tried to domesticate these birds—with

FIG. 17
E. Riou, *Iguasa Tender,*
Near Tuluá, 1875–76

only partial success—so that they would not be just an occasional dish, when the iguasas arrived by the thousands at harvest time, but rather everyday fare. The position of iguasa herder arose thanks to the challenge of this hunt, as well as out of widespread appreciation for the delicate meat.[53]

Something else happens where big game hunting is concerned. When chasing and capturing a bear, for instance, one must organize a hunting party with horses, dogs, and spears and be willing to risk one's life when the animal, cornered and furious, decides to confront its pursuers. Mollien, in his *Viaje por la República de Colombia* (Voyage through the Republic of Colombia), tells of one of these incidents:

In these wild regions the hunter chases animals that, surrounded by eternal mist, think they are safe from man's weapons. The bear that lives there is known for its ferocity and strength. The inhabitants of the region hunt it only now and then. Mounted on horseback and armed with spears, they attack it and sometimes manage to kill it, a feat not without its dangers. It is a curious spectacle, at such a considerable altitude, to hear the cries of the hunters, the howls of the dogs, and all the clamor of the hunt to be suddenly replaced, smothered, by the whistle of the wind, but, especially, what cannot be seen without wonder is the galloping of the horsemen, completely fearless, along these escarped peaks, crossing the torrents at full speed, eschewing the precipices, scaling the rocks and, finally, spearing the animal, which, exhausted from fleeing, faces them down.[54]

This task generally begins early, when the peasants discover one of these bears roaming near their cultivated fields. While the hunters are being organized, the bear must be kept at bay, and then begins the long and exhausting chase up the mountain. They will return in the late afternoon, tired and sweaty, with the prey if things have gone well and, on not a few occasions, with one or two fewer dogs— or perhaps a wounded or dead companion. There is nothing recreational about the task of hunting. Even Efraín's father, in the novel *María*, maintains that in his country—Jamaica—bear hunting was considered a "savage" job. What happens, in the case at hand, is that these "savages" are obliged to engage in the demanding hunt using unreliable weapons, because to do otherwise would be equivalent to letting their harvests be destroyed and placing their families in grave peril. The entire bear would be utilized. Its fat would be turned into lard, used as a remedy for arthritic or muscular aches; its meat, like pork, would be appreciated by the servants, especially the meat of the soles of the paws; and the hide would be tanned for sale at market or be used as a rug in the homes of the estate owners.

In *María* we have, in addition, the hunt of a jaguar. This is a project for the peasants, who have seen their flocks of lambs dwindle because of the animal's voraciousness. One of the peasants who live in the foothills invites Efraín, the *patroncito* (young master), to join them. This is done as a sign of respect but also out of necessity, for he is the only one who has a reliable firearm. In this way we begin to understand the different attitudes toward hunting on the part of slaves and peasants, on the one hand, and that of masters and powerful landowners, on the other. For the former it is a task both indispensable and dangerous, for the latter an activity that borders on sport. Although still risky, the activity acquires the character of a virile pastime, for the modern weapon grants appreciable advantages over the predator. For Fernández-Armesto, hunting among the upper classes has the "aristocratic aftertaste of the pursuit through the forest or the chase across the plain, the free-fall descent of the falcon, or the jaguar's leap toward freedom."[55] Efraín even shows a certain disdain for one member of the hunting party who suffers an instant of panic at the point of confronting the corralled beast.

FIG. 18
E. Riou, *Hunting a Jaguar in El Quindío*, 1875–76

The truth is that, except for Efraín, the four remaining hunters find themselves practically helpless. Each one carries an antiquated hunting pistol, which fails just when it is most needed. Even those who manage to fire their weapons barely provoke superficial wounds in the animal, such that the only consequence is to make it more dangerous. Only two of the four carry spears over their shoulders.

Hunting the jaguar takes time; it entails covering rugged mountainous terrain and facing serious risks. The hunt reaches its culminating moment when the hunters and dogs manage to surround the wounded feline, which hastens to defend itself from their attacks. Isaacs narrates the climax as follows:

Of the six dogs, two were already hors de combat: one of them lying mangled at the feet of the fierce animal; the other, with its entrails protruding from

FIG. 19 E. Riou, *Jaguar*, 1875–76

between broken ribs, had come to find us and, giving forth the most heart-rending cries, died at the foot of the rock on which we had climbed.

With his side turned to a clump of oaks, his tail playing about like a serpent, his back erect, his eyes flaming, and his teeth bared, the jaguar was uttering hoarse cries, and as he threw his enormous head about, his ears made a noise something like castanets.[56]

Then comes the final attack, and, as may be expected, one of the peasants "aimed [his gun], but the only thing that burned was the wick"; another, his spear broken, was left at the jaguar's mercy, and Efraín, the novel's hero, tells us, "My rifle alone was available. I fired. The jaguar slumped backward, reeled, and fell."[57] The young master dispatched the wild beast with one sharp shot "between the eyes" and, besides, saved the life of one of the hunters who was defenseless before the predator. Of course, this all forms part of the atmosphere the novelist creates to aggrandize his masculine protagonist. But the difference in attitudes as to the hunt does not fail to be reflected in the novel's text.

The masters praise their weapons. Carlos, Efraín's friend who arrives after the jaguar hunt, for example, laments the fact that he did not have a chance to try his new "English shotgun." He unpacks and shows it to Efraín, who comments on its being "precisely like the one my father had given me on my return from Bogotá." The conversation between the two has something of a competitive and arrogant tone, in which each young man seems to measure his importance by the quality and novelty of his weapon. To be sure, hunting is for them no sacrifice. In fact, when Carlos demands that Efraín organize another hunt, Efraín's sister tells him, "He will be much pleased to *gratify* you," with which she makes explicit the character that this activity has for the elite groups: the hunt as a diversion, rather than as a necessity, which is the nature of the matter from the standpoint of the subordinate social groups.[58]

The slaves and peasants have no occasion to brag. Some of them will even flee in fear, for the hunt is barely another item in the long daily grind, and, when dangerous wild animals are concerned, they know they are at a disadvantage and are running risks. There is not much space for fantasizing between one hunt and the next, for the time will be occupied by the toil of country life. It is one more task, but more demanding than most, and surely, for them, it does not belong to the world of play.

Even with this difference between master and slave, it is perhaps the only aspect of cooking (including fishing, as has already been explained) that has an exclusively masculine character.[59] It is the counterpart, in the world of cuisine, of culinary preparation, which turns out to be the almost exclusive domain of women. Other tasks—sowing, reaping, selling, collecting wild berries, and so on—are shared between the genders.

Of the different components of the cultural world of the kitchen—acquiring, processing, distributing, preserving, preparing, and consuming the food—hunting, as a form of acquisition, is the one that plays a significant role in the novel of Isaacs, both for reasons related to the plot and for the general focus of the text. It expresses a longing for a lost time, one in which masculine superiority ruled, narrated from the perspective of paternal authority. Even so, we can glimpse, in that very same realm, that there is also a popular perspective, one opposed to that expressed by the narrator and more useful when it comes to evaluating the role of cooking in the cultural formation of a given region of Latin America in the middle of the nineteenth century, when the slaveholding estate reigned supreme.

Just as in all aspects of the kitchen, the hunt has a symbolic meaning. Here is how Mintz formulates it: "Eating is never a purely biological activity. . . . Meals have a history associated with those who consume them; the techniques employed to obtain them, process them, prepare them, serve them, and consume them are always variable, culturally speaking, and they also have their own history. Meals are not just eating; their consumption is always conditioned by their meaning. These meanings are symbolic, and they are communicated symbolically."[60]

That explains why Lévi-Strauss considers the kitchen to be a semantic field in the form of a triangle whose three angles correspond, respectively, to the categories of the raw, the cooked, and the rotten.[61] The cooked is the cultural transformation of the raw, while the rotten is its natural transformation. That is the source of his binary oppositions between roasted and cooked, natural and

FIG. 20 *Sale of African Slaves*, 1836

cultivated, masculine and feminine, nomadic and sedentary, aristocratic and popular, prodigal and frugal, and exquisite versus common. In this symbolic space the hunt corresponds to the masculine and is associated with the first terms in the chain of oppositions: it is natural, masculine, nomadic, aristocratic, prodigal, and exquisite. It is superior to cooking, which pertains to women. It is closer to the raw and associated with the roasted, with the techniques of the outdoor barbecue and large chunks of bloody meat that successful hunters consume. It is the space of masculine taste and male companionship.

These values apply in *María* after the jaguar hunt. The hunters gather in an opening in the woods, relaxed and satisfied. They are alone and victorious, and the closest au naturel kitchen takes over: "The huge knives came out of their sheaths. José cut up the meat for us, and this, with the corn, made a dish fit for a king. We drank up the wine, made havoc with the bread, and finished the figs and cherries, which were more to the taste of my companions than to mine. . . . My best cigars ended the rustic banquet."[62]

It is a symbolically male kitchen: roast meat—even if, in this case, it was not cooked by them—amid the toil of the hunt, without the affectations of a set table, and rustic. But, at the same time, the kitchen was regal, with not just any common cuisine but rather a banquet, aristocratic and superior.

FIG. 21 E. Riou, *Roasting a Tapir*, 1883

This symbolic power of the kitchen is what explains that even today occasions of roasts and preparations on the barbecue grill continue to be spaces of male involvement in most cultures, no matter if we are in a shopping mall in Cali or any old Sunday on the patio of the home of a family in the south of Brazil. In *María* the distinction is sharp: hunting is a man's work, just as the components of the kitchen belong to the realm of women. At the hunting party women are not welcome.

Traditional Cooking and Hunger

Right there, as you can see, he doesn't lack for his eight good
cows, his herd of swine, his little farm, and two good mares.
. . . He is the son of a mulatto woman who cost the old man
plenty . . . , because only four months after he'd bought her in
Quilachao, she went and died on him.

—Isaacs, *María*, 144

Haven't I seen you eat one of my stews with relish? The only
trouble is it isn't done yet.

—Isaacs, *María*, 148

It is cleverly said that in the valley of the Cauca River three patron saints rule: San Jon, San Cudo, and San Cocho (properly *zanjón, zancudo,* and sancocho). The first is a type of long trench filled with water, the second is a mosquito that carries malaria and announces its presence with an annoying buzz as it pulsates in the American tropics, and the third is the dish par excellence of the masses that populate various Latin American regions. The three are united: the water, always abundant in equatorial lands, contributes to the formation of trenches and different types of topographies in which it pools; constant water and heat are a source of a diversity of species and the favorite habitat of numerous swarms of insects, among other creatures; and incessant heat and humidity explain the abundance of life forms that are typical and permit the creation of that hearty stew called sancocho, which involves meats, tubers, vegetables, spices, and condiments.

Sancocho is, at one and the same time, a dish that symbolizes diversity and the everyday. A mixture of different ingredients simmered for long periods of time, it has its forebears among both the Iberian peoples and pre-Hispanic communities. It is the heir of the legendary *olla podrida,* whose roots run deep in the Iberian Peninsula, and *locro,* which was habitual fare among the peoples of the Inca Empire.[63] There are as many variants of it as there are ethnic hybrids in Latin America's multiple habitats. We thus have Dominican, Ecuadorian, Colombian, Venezuelan, Panamanian, and even—going beyond the hemisphere—Canary Island sancocho, and, called by a different name, *ajiaco* in Cuba, Chile, and Colombia. By the same token, in each of the regions of these countries, sancocho manifests individual characteristics associated with the foods produced in the territory and the cultural features predominant in the racial mixing. Strictly speaking, as a preparation common to the cuisine of a good part of Latin America, sancocho is "without borders," for it surpasses geographic or political boundaries. It is therefore inaccurate to consider it the national dish of any country—setting aside the difficulties inherent in such a notion of national cuisines. At most, one can settle on a regional denomination, focusing on the small differences in ingredients found in the distinct geographic locales. But the basic culinary procedures are the same for vast areas of the subcontinent. Rather than a differentiating element among peoples and communities, sancocho is an expression of Latin American cultural unity.

The only one of its ingredients that comes to be indispensable is meat: game, fish, or domestic animals of any sort. Nonetheless, it is beef, meat of the *Bos taurus* brought over by the Spanish conquistadors, that has dominated over a long period of time. In fact, it is around beef that most of Latin American culinary culture develops. In the singular universe of the kitchens in *María,* meat is synonymous with beef. And sancocho is the preferred and most common way to cook it.

Not just any cut of meat will do, but corned or jerked beef—that is, meat preserved by salting and hanging it exposed to the elements so that the sun and wind, together with the salt, cause it to dehydrate and permit it to keep without spoiling. Historically, it was also smoked, placed in wooden boxes over a charcoal barbecue. In fact, people preferred the meat preserved that way to eating it fresh, for it lent more flavor to the sancocho. And this did not apply just to the Creoles. A Spanish priest, Friar Juan de Santa Gertrudis, who frequented part of the territories located to the south of the setting of *María*, relates the following: "I arrived at the house, which belonged to a man of mixed race, and I asked him if he would sell me fifty pounds of meat. He answered that he would. He weighed out fifty pounds of pork, the most beautiful thing I have ever seen, having those long white streaks of interspersed fat you find in bacon. Its mere fragrance made you hungry. . . . The slices were just salted . . . , but they appeared to be so well cured that they caused no repugnance whatsoever, as might a slice of raw ham upon eating."[64]

The characteristic flavor of the sancocho came from the meat subjected to a double process of transformation: first dehydration and curing and then cooking it over a low flame accompanied by vegetables, tubers, and spices. In the Cauca River Valley, it was typical to mix it with scallions, garlic, Mexican oregano and cilantro for flavor and aroma, plantain and yucca as fillers and thickeners, and corn on the cob, cooked separately and added at the end, just before serving. Of course, in keeping with the democratic spirit of the culinary setting, other ingredients could be welcome, such as winter squash in the Cauca Valley, yam in different parts of the Caribbean, and *malanga* or Chinese potatoes on the Colombian Pacific coast. Also, when it was possible, other meats and even other vegetables were added. Sancocho is a sort of culinary allegory of Latin American culture. For Fernando Ortiz, for example, the essence of the Cuban character is expressed, above all, through ajiaco, which is the very same sancocho we are discussing.[65] The same could be said about the essence of the Colombian character, the Ecuadorian, the Peruvian, and so on, except that by this means you don't achieve any distinction at all, since sancocho or ajiaco is a dish common to all.

With sancocho as a foundation, one can reconstruct not only the history of the culture of broad regions of Latin America but their economic history as well—and even the local particularities of the economy, when one concentrates on ingredients proper to microclimates or varying altitudes. The Cauca Valley speaks to an agrarian world dominated by cattle herding and the cultivation of plantain, yucca, and corn. It introduces us to large livestock pastures in the bottom land along the Cauca River, in which sizable herds of cattle grazed at will; it speaks to us of the small landholdings in which "he doesn't lack for his eight good cows, his herd of swine . . . and two good mares," as Isaacs says in *María*.[66] The author reveals to us a population of herdsmen, dedicated part of the time to dairy farming, a lariat in one hand and an obedient horse as a mount;

he even permits us to glimpse the outlines of settlements and social strata as regards that life of meadows and muleteers.

Despite the relevance of the foregoing, however, the habitat of the kitchens of *María* was something more than plains, and its economy, more than cattle husbandry. We are dealing with one of the natural spaces of the greatest biodiversity on the planet. Humboldt called it the "splendid Cauca River Valley," and a pair of peasants who functioned as local authorities, Fernando de Colonia and Juan Nicolás de Urdinola, wrote this to the king of Spain, at the dawn of the nineteenth century:

> The settlers are in general inclined to raise crops, such as the cacao plants that grow in greater or lesser quantity. . . . Besides this plant they have innumerable banana plantations, and they raise many swine. . . . Without interrupting planting cycles, they plant many rows of maize, ñames, arrowroot, watermelons, musk melons, pumpkins, yams, *sidrayotas* [popularly called the "poor man's potato"], onions, tomatoes, chili peppers, lettuce, cabbage, radishes, grapefruits, potatoes, chickpeas, *pallar* beans, anise, mustard, barley, bananas, sugarcane . . . quinine for medicine, borage, dill, cilantro, parsley, oregano, lindl, *escancer* [a red wild bean], grass, chamomile, wild musk, roses, tamarinds, drumstick trees, mallow, *tavera* beans, wormwood [*Chenopodium ambroidoides*], and many other plants that remain unlisted because their names are unknown.

They indicate the captive farming of "deer, *guaguas*, guatines [a small mammal], and rabbits." And they write about the swine heart of palm, noting that "when it is ripe, the seasoned heart of this bunch, which because the swine feed on it is called 'swine heart,' is enjoyed in its skin and the inner stone that is eventually shed. The inhabitants artfully concoct a kind of butter from this heart, nobler and subtler than the oil of the olive . . . , agreeable to the palate for all sorts of meals."[67]

Finally, they add, "There are also the coconut palm trees . . . , custard apples, acidics, hearts of palm, sweet and sour limes, oranges . . . , guavas, cider, passion fruit, papayas, *papayuelas* [*Caricacea pubescens*], alligator pears, pomegranates, avocados, all edible tree fruits. Common animals, chickens, turkeys, ducks, wild swan, peacocks, *coclíes* [like the heron but larger], *cucharo* ducks, pink ducks, herons, teals, iguasa ducks, all edible. . . . Edible four-legged animals include the peccary, *tatabro* [a mammal like a small deer], capybara [*Hydrochoerus hydrochaeris*], iguana, armadillo, tortoise."[68] There were as many kinds of sancocho, then, as animals available. And, in view of religious prohibitions, fish sancocho, almost always made of bocachico, was also common during periods of fasting, as well as sancocho made with aquatic mammals and even rabbit, because of the priests' mistaken belief that these were not "meat."[69]

An inseparable companion of meat, both in sancocho and in other culinary preparations of the American tropics, was—and still is—the plantain, a fruit whose abundance has often been noted. As we saw, Fernando de Colonia and Juan Nicolás de Urdinola signal that the plantain groves were "innumerable," and Víctor Manuel Patiño states how "plantain spread with great speed and was used not only as a fruit but also in the preparation of drinks and vinegar."[70] A food intimately linked with the Afro-descendant population, even though it was brought from the Canary Islands by the Spaniards, it was the "daily bread" in the kitchens of *María*, cooked in multiple forms, green, pintón (partially ripe), and mature; processed as flour; or eaten raw. The identification of the plantain, especially green, with the people of the Cauca Valley was so great that they were called by the nickname *biche* by their neighbors along the boundary with Antioquia.[71]

In the closing years of the nineteenth century, when the novel *María* was causing a furor on the continent and its author was receiving his just renown, the physician Evaristo García studied the importance of the plantain in the diet of this tropical region of America, and he underscored sancocho as a dish of great nutritional value. Although it is not his main interest, he cannot but explain to us how to prepare sancocho the way it was done by the black cooks in his family's home in the city of Cali:

> To prepare a good sancocho, you place to boil in two or three liters of water a spongy chunk of cow bone and several pieces of fatty meat, which together weigh four hundred or five hundred grams. Little by little, over a low flame, the water softens the meat in the ceramic pot; you then add the plantain broken into pieces with the fingertips, after cleaning the peeled fruit in cold water to remove the astringent stain of the covering, and add to it chunks of yucca and calabash or squash. Salt is added from the beginning in sufficient quantity to give flavor to the broth, along with some other exciting condiments, such as onion, parsley, or cilantro. Be sure to stir the contents steadily as they boil so they absorb the flavors. The boiling water evaporates until the resulting paste lends a certain fluid density to the broth, and the pieces of softened plantain grow tender by the action of the fire and mix with the stew. Cooked in this manner, sancocho is a complete food, easy to digest.[72]

He also mentions a popular type of sancocho, common to a peasant style of eating, called "cowboy sancocho," which features the combination of "green plantain; dried, salted meat; and cilantro" and is customary to "satisfy the accumulated hunger of the peons, travelers, and cattle drivers."[73] Studious and well informed about the details of living conditions of the different classes of the period, he observes how in the region he inhabits "there are still large stretches of virgin forest" and impenetrable terrain in which "yucca, corn, cacao, sugarcane, tobacco, and a diversity of edible fruits are produced." He notes further that he has traveled through the forests of the Cauca Valley "and, where one might expect to find virgin forest, we have found inhabitants of the Ethiopian race, living in straw huts, situated amid plantain trees and other useful vegetation." He indicates, additionally, that several of these settler families of the periphery "also possess pastureland and heads of horses, cattle, and swine," allowing him to conclude that the "Cauca Valley, in the entire river basin, is one of the regions most favored by Providence to wage the struggle for survival."

What García discovers, upon examining the dietary habits of the Cauca Valley population, is that—without understanding it but observing empirically—this community has found a combination of foods in which the plantain plays a major role and "serves to regenerate the fabric and to produce heat and mechanical force." For the European-educated physician, "The peasant workers in the Cauca Valley are in general robust men who can withstand eight or nine hours of work daily, but serious work, with hatchet in hand, felling forests, and they don't feed themselves on more than a modest ration of plantain, meat, and salt."

This nutritional regimen grants them advantages of output over the European laborer, he affirms, as well as over the inhabitants of the mountains and semitropical highlands. What happens is that hunger has no place in the poverty of this region. In reality, when we examine the living conditions of the Cauca Valley populations in the nineteenth century, and even at the start of the twentieth, leaving aside the hardest years of the Wars of Independence or the episodic eruptions of the locust plague, we find that the poor who inhabit the spaces of *María* suffer from everything but a lack of food. They lack money, solid housing, education, health care, clothes, proper hunting or work implements, and so on, but never an abundant and steaming bowl of sancocho on the table. That is how the fiction of Isaacs tells it, for not even in the humblest of kitchens would meat—beef, pork, or fish—be absent, nor would plantain or other ingredients that attest to the wealth and diversity of the traditional cuisine.

Even Félix Serret, a French traveler who visited the same territory in the second decade of the twentieth century as part of a journey throughout Colombia, confirmed the abundance enjoyed in the Cauca Valley. He mentions the "immense natural meadows where herds of bovines grazed in complete freedom . . . , marshes where innumerable herons mixed their brilliant colors with the aquatic flowers . . . , sugarcane or banana plantations, amid which suddenly appeared rustic living quarters, animated in their surroundings by groups of kids, completely naked, who played the whole blessed day with the dogs, ducks, and piglets."[74]

The situation of nutritional security led the French government functionary, a severe critic of the Colombian upper classes and their bureaucracy, to go to the extreme of recalling "our working families who suffer such travails to feed and raise their own" and of questioning his own modernity: "I ask myself, therefore, upon seeing these little black children, playing along the banks of the Cauca so carefree with their dogs and little pigs, if it wouldn't be better for them and for the others to never become acquainted with our carnivalesque styles, our complicated cuisine, our adulterated liqueurs, our homicidal carriages, and the entire useless claptrap of our modern luxury."[75]

Old ideas of Jean-Jacques Rousseau's *Emile* and the noble savage abound in these considerations of the Gallic traveler.[76] But there is no doubt that these and other observations of very different individuals agree in identifying the absence of hunger as a condition that curiously coexists with poverty in the culinary space of *María*. Research more intensely focused on the economic regime, system of private property, demography, and rural labor—all beyond the aims of this text— would show how the traditional universe of the slaveholding estate, combined with a periphery of small landholdings and free spaces in forested zones, created conditions that eliminated hunger and made effective use of the region's surprising biodiversity. Given that, it is also undeniably true that the system promoted social inequality and maintained a status quo of numerous inequities, but the absence of hunger in and of itself remains an important achievement. Beyond Isaacs's own childhood remembrances, the nostalgia in his novel for this world gone by is, then, justified by being based in fact.

The same happened in other regions of Latin America that had similar environments. Lovera, in his *Historia de la alimentación en Venezuela* (History of eating in Venezuela), speaks of a "golden age of eating" in certain regions, connected to the "traditional Creole alimentary regime," configured in the first half of the eighteenth century, which "lasted for almost two centuries."[77] He ascertains the calories of the habitual diet among poor rural workers, concludes that it was quite a bit higher than the minimum nutritional requirements, and supports his affirmations with a good number of primary sources. Among these sources we find the suggestive observation of the German explorer Karl F. Appun, who traveled through there in 1849:

Meat is the daily watchword in Venezuela, as is beer in Bavaria. Whoever might try to change the price of meat in that country would arouse the ire of the entire population, I mean martyrdom, with the same certainty as when the human monster might dare raise the price of beer by one Kreutzer in Bavaria. . . . Salted meat, fried meat, stewed meat, three times a day, that is how the daily Venezuelan menu reads, and that is what everyone expects and demands. It is thus very true that a native-born Venezuelan could hardly live, or at least would find his existence challenged, without his daily dose of sancocho and roasted plantains.

Another observer, the Englishman Edward Sullivan, a traveler in Venezuela in 1851, confirms the inexistence of hunger among the poor population, as well as the modesty of the wealth among the few people of means, and he indicates that "limitless beef can be obtained here at just a half penny per pound, and the plantains and bananas almost for nothing at all."[78]

Of course, sancocho is the dish that embodies this well-being. It signals that food self-sufficiency and explains its character—autonomous, rebellious, and running counter to authority—as a noteworthy trait in the behavior of the Cauca Valley peasants, and it even explains the weak links between masters and slaves in the final periods of the slave regime. The frequent complaints of the authorities about the chronic rule breaking; the massive evasion of paying taxes and of obeying laws, especially in the cases of the production of tobacco and brandy; the scolding by the priests for poor attendance at Mass; the proliferation of cohabitation outside wedlock—in short, all these shows of independence in behavior among the Cauca Valley poor—would have no explanation without considering the possibility of acquiring, through their own efforts, their "daily bread." To parody the old refrain, if it is true that man does not live by sancocho alone, it is also true, to a greater degree, that without sancocho he could not live at all. Knowing that one may satisfy one's essential human needs by turning to the diversity and abundance of the environment, without depending on authorities or patrons, even if that may require long and hard days' toil, allows one to put aside other necessities, even if some of them may be vital, and grants people the free spirit in which they revel.

The foregoing also means that sancocho is a symbol for entire ways of life. When García calls a popular dish "cowboy sancocho," referring to the more common kind, that which has as its base beef and plantain, he alludes to the male space of cooking, which, in almost every case, is found in the process of acquiring those foodstuffs. Livestock is a man's thing. One finds there a world of male superiority where what matters is the ability to lasso a calf on the gallop, take down a weaned heifer with one's bare hands, cape a bull in the festivities of the arena, or castrate an unbroken colt without letting the wound bleed or get infected. As in the hunt, the presence of women is prohibited, unless they serve as milkmaids.

On the other hand, even if it is the cowboy sort, the other components of cooking sancocho bring it within a woman's domain. She prepares the jerky, cultivates the plantain grove and the orchard, and watches over the culinary procedure that will convert this simple and familiar victual into a nutritious dish of delicately balanced flavor. "Haven't I seen you eat one of my stews with relish?" Salomé's mother asks Efraín, in a sentence referring to sancocho that is an indication, at one and the same time, of humility and pride.[79] It is an expression of her effort and her expertise in the job she does best. It is what makes her indispensable, for her mastery is what sustains the family and ensures its survival. In sanco-cho the contributions of common women and men are combined, and, in a way, it constitutes a demonstration of the disposable nature of the small group of men and women of the elite. The truth is that they in no way contributed to its creation and perfection. On the contrary, as one gathers from the references of the physician García, the role of the upper class should be sought simply in the modification of tradition and taste.[80]

EPILOGUE
Cooking and Culture

In view of the difficulties entailed in reaching a universally accepted concept of culture, perhaps the most useful perspective may be to consider it as an assemblage of human actions and meanings, integrated by a series of basic elements or subassemblages: languages, eating customs, ideologies, transformations of the habitat, and the extremely important aspects of clothing, ornamentation, and sexuality.

As with all combinations—when not a matter of a pedagogical model—its elements never appear in a pure form, in a state of singularity, but rather exist interrelated, contaminated by one another, in permanent movement and, even, each becoming the other. That is why the study of culture is impossible without the collaboration of various disciplines and the adoption of multiple perspectives.

Any one of the basic elements of culture calls for specialized knowledge in so many different fields that they exceed the abilities of the lone scholar. Human languages, for example, lead us back to speech, tongues, oral narrations, writing, literature, music, nonverbal communication, graphic or pictorial representations, and so on. And each one of these fields opens onto a whole range of specialties that require varied expertise, as any literary professional knows, not to mention the linguists or musicologists. The same thing happens with each of the other elements and, of course, and with more reason, with culture as the combination that spans and integrates them all.

The contaminated nature of each element gives it its cultural character or, better still, makes it a fact of culture. A novel is not merely literature, just as the cult to the Virgin Mary is not merely religion, nor is an electoral proclamation merely politics, or a building exclusively architecture. Each is that and much more. Neither is it the sum of its component parts but rather a knot of meanings that, to complicate the matter further, moves and discloses itself in ceaseless transformation.

That is why cultural analysis, whether the study of the history of culture in a determined human aggregation or the interpretation of a literary text or the criticism of certain pictorial movements cannot help but refer to basic elements that constitute it, or its dynamic, and this requires disciplinary cooperation. But it also necessitates that we resign ourselves to a knowledge that is approximate and relative, since each cultural fact is such because it is composed of heterogeneity, because it alludes to other things, because it moves between fields distant from one another, at least in perception. That coming and going, those threads of reference that shakily cross and the plotting of meanings that they construct make it impossible to apprehend the cultural fact in its totality, since each time we approach it and think we have encompassed it, it has already changed and begun to manifest itself in a different way. It is not so much a useless task as an endless one.

These reflections have guided my effort to "know in depth the nature and needs of the people," as Bello sought, from the perspective of their eating habits.[1] They show the possibilities of the chosen focus and explain the need to appeal to history, anthropology, culinary techniques, and the link between them and social relations. They also reveal the insoluble difficulties that confront authors when they adopt a cultural standpoint in a state of insularity. Despite its limitations, this type of work can make evident aspects that, from another angle, would pass unnoticed or scarcely be glimpsed. We will always achieve better results when interdisciplinary teams approach cultural facts from the multiple, but integrated, viewpoints they demand.

NOTES

· ·

Author's Preface

1. Romoli, *Colombia*, 3–4.
2. Ibid., 20.
3. Ortiz, *Contrapunteo cubano*, 96.
4. Malinowski, prologue to Ortiz, *Contrapunteo cubano*, 4–5.
5. Patiño Ossa, "Estado natural de la libertad," 26–43.
6. Translator's note: One of the distinct advantages of translating the works of living authors lies in the possibility of consulting with them over thorny linguistic or cultural problems. *Chuyaco* is a term that lay beyond my personal experience, and it was nowhere to be found in dictionaries or web searches. To my query as to the meaning of this term, the author responded with the Spanish equivalent of what follows:
Chuyaco is an untranslatable term. Of Quechua origin, *yaco* means "water," while the prefix *Chu* denotes insecurity, thus rendering uncertain the quality of what is affirmed immediately thereafter. The expression refers to a family of liquid foods, proper to pre-Hispanic cooking, two of which are *chicha*—fermented corn combined with water and honey—and *champús*: grains of white corn cooked and combined with fruit juices (of *lulo* [in Cauca Country], pineapple [in Cartagena], or *guanabana* [in Lima]) mixed with brown sugar, *achiote*, and chopped cilantro. The term constitutes a question: Is it water or not? Could it be cold soup or fruit salad? Is it a drink or a meal?
7. See Patiño Ossa, "Bienmesabe vallecaucano."

Preamble

1. Transculturation is a concept championed by the Cuban polymath Fernando Ortiz and Uruguayan literary critic Angel Rama regarding the mutual effects that different cultures have on one another, even when one culture may be politically dominant. For example, whereas the Spanish conquerors were able to impose slavery on the manacled and uprooted Africans and to build an empire on their virtually free labor, those subjugated peoples were able to institute forms of music, dance, cuisine, religion, and so on that permeate the shared culture and endure to this day.
2. Hamilton, *Viajes por el interior*, 232, 255.
3. Ibid., 311. Fufú is part of a forgotten feast. *Bala* from Tumaco, made from cooked green bananas salted to taste, puréed and mixed in a base of *achiote* and diluted in abundant butter with a tinge of smashed garlic, perhaps gives a hint of the idea. There also exists a compound variant, called *bala marinera* (*bala a la marinara*), in which a layer of this dough is covered with briefly scalded shrimp in *hogao* cream sauce with coconut milk and a bit of *pique*. This is all covered with another layer of fufú, to form beautifully colored squares that are served as appetizers. The fufú mentioned by Isaacs in *María* replaces butter with a "substantial broth," which could be meat- or fish-based, according to whatever was served as the main dish. Lovera calls it fufú, and he identifies it as a recipe proper to West Africa and the source of *cafunga*, an everyday dish among the black population of Barlovento, in Venezuela (*Gastronomía caribeña*, 55; see glossary for italicized terms).
4. Dumas, *Grand dictionnaire de cuisine*.
5. Pérez, *Guía del buen comer español*, 63.
6. We are dealing with Friar Juan de Santa Gertrudis, who tells of it in *Maravillas de la naturaleza*, 2:221.

7. Hamilton, *Viajes por el interior*, 260.

8. This freshwater turtle, known popularly as the *bache*, of whose abundance in rivers, marshes, and swamps there are innumerable references, is now almost extinct, not because of excessive harvesting on the part of the peasants but because of the contamination of the tributaries of the Cauca River from agro-industrial development and because of the effects of draining marshes and swamps. Fortunately, of late the CVC (Cauca Valley Corporation, an environmental agency established in the 1950s by the United States has initiated a repopulation of the species in sites such as La Humareda swamp in the environs of the municipality of Bolívar. Farming them is the way for this traditional soup to again form part of our diet.

9. Hamilton cites Humboldt, when the latter writes, "It would be worthwhile to make the trip to Popayán, just to have the pleasure of eating custard apples." For the Englishman this fruit is "exquisitely flavorful, much like a mixture of strawberries, cream, and sugar" (*Viajes por el interior*, 234–35).

10. Hamilton observes, "The Indians also bring from the headwaters of the Puracé River abundant loads of snow. . . . Ice cream vendors can be seen on the streets" (*Viajes por el interior*).

11. Quevedo, quoted in Patiño, *Del condumio y del yantar*, 44.

12. In the case of the Cauca River Valley, the racial mixing especially takes the form of a large mulatto population. See Patiño Ossa, "Raíces de africanía."

13. Juan Bautista Sardella, *Relación del descubrimiento de las provincias de Antioquia por Jorge Robledo* (Report on the discovery of the provinces of Antioquia by Jorge Robledo), cited by Patiño Ossa, *Herr Simmonds*.

14. Yanacona is a Quechua-derived word whose meaning is "servant." The Yanaconas were originally individuals in the Inca Empire who worked at a variety of tasks for the Inca, his family, or the religious establishment. When the Spanish conquistadors arrived in modern-day Peru, the Yanaconas declared themselves "friends of the Spaniards" and assisted the Spaniards in taking control of the empire. Sebastián de Belalcázar (1479–1551), a Spanish conquistador who founded the city of Cali and in the 1530s conquered the Cauca River Valley, had brought more than three thousand Yanaconas with him from Peru when he arrived in present-day Colombia.

15. One of the reasons was the difficult process of colonization in the Cauca Valley region, which complicated the livestock's acclimatization. In contrast to what happened in the Pubenza Valley and in the highlands of Nariño, the indigenous communities of this area fought tenaciously, almost to extinction, and the survivors chose to flee toward the forests of the Pacific coast rather than be subjected to the Spanish masters. Reminiscent of the Spanish Conquest, the wars, uprooting of settlements, battles, and massacres continued well into the seventeenth century. See Valencia Llanos, *Resistencia militar indígena*.

16. Cieza de León, *Crónica del Perú*, 112–13.

17. Patiño, *Del condumio y del yantar*, 514, 519, 522, 539.

18. Riofrío is today a municipality on the west bank of the Cauca River, toward the northern end of the Departamento del Valle, abutting the Departamento del Chocó.

19. Bocachico were and still are considered commonplace. Nonetheless, because of their abundance and capacity to produce fat, they are most probably gorrones, which saved the Spaniards in the first years of the conquest and are most popular in the Cauca Valley fish sancocho. They also produce delicacies. A few years ago a lady from Villacolombia (a lower-class neighborhood in Cali) chose large-size male bocachicos, fileted them, and smoked them over a fire of corncobs with herbs she kept secret, until they cooked in their own fat and took on an attractive golden color. These filets presented in that way make a dish for the most demanding of palates. In the marketplace of Florida (a hamlet in the Cauca Valley) an old black cook would remove the eggs from the female bocachicos, salt them, soak them in coconut milk, tie them tightly in plantain leaves, and cook them until they curdled. Then she uncovered them and roasted them over a wood fire oven until they were golden and the coconut milk was reduced to a cream. She called it bocachico bread, and the process produces an extremely fine paté.

20. García, *Escritos escogidos*, 132–33.

21. Hamilton, *Viajes por el interior*, 312.

22. Where frying technique is concerned—and not just that of fish—mastery belongs to the descendants of female slaves: knowing the temperature of the oil, when a variety should be breaded or not, and when the breading consists barely of dropping it in flour or when, because of the meat's delicacy, it merits a bath in flour and egg. Back in the valley of old, when wheat was scarce, the breading was of ground and moistened rice, which produces a crunchier and subtler texture, to which we should perhaps return.

23. Hamilton, *Viajes por el interior*, 293.

24. Cieza de León, *Crónica del Perú*, 110

25. Patiño, *Relaciones de vísperas*, 34, 41.

26. Pérez, *Guía del buen comer español*, 270–71.

27. Palacios, *Alférez real*, 107; Barney Cabrera, *Notas y apostillas*, 107.

28. Patiño, *Relaciones de vísperas*, 373–92.

29. Holton, *Nueva Granada*, 144.

30. As a note of curiosity, a recipe is given for cheesecake that was prepared on an estate near the same hamlet of Florida in the 1950s and that, according to the old cook, was a family recipe from long ago. The batter was made from wheat flour; filled with a mixture of fresh cheese, sugar, and whole eggs; perfumed with *yerbabuena* leaves; and baked in a wood-fire oven. Customary during Holy Week, it was a delicious treat that spread its aroma. Dionisio Pérez, in his very useful *Guía del buen comer español* (Guide to good Spanish eating), refers to a similar cake, in the old gastronomy of the Balearic and Canary Islands, which reveals ancient influences of Arabs, Africans, and Americans. Much of Canary cuisine integrated easily into our cooking (316).

31. Isaacs, *María*, 37 (my translation; all page references to Isaacs's novel correspond to the Biblioteca Ayacucho edition, edited by Gustavo Mejía, which encompasses changes that Isaacs himself made after the original 1867 edition of *María* found such international success).

32. Patiño, *Relaciones de vísperas*, 295.

33. Its preparation would be learned in a singular manner, which is no longer done: the bitter chocolate is cooked in fresh sugarcane juice. The result is magnificent in taste and texture.

34. Patiño, *Relaciones de vísperas*.

35. Cieza de León, *Crónica del Perú*, 141.

36. Ibid., 115.

37. Patiño Ossa, "Raíces de africanía," 40.

38. Barney Cabrera, *Notas y apostillas*, 82.

39. Ibid., 24.

40. See ibid., 43–44.

41. This recipe, which is the most reminiscent of our own, in agreement with Dionisio Pérez, was made in a glazed ceramic pot, with beef and pork, along with a head of garlic, clove, and saffron, and was topped off with chunks of cabbage, squash, sweet potato, potato, and an ear of corn (*Guía del buen comer español*, 318). It is also interesting to note that in the Canary Islands it is customary to find "seven-meat stew," obligatory for wedding banquets, in which pork, beef, chicken, rabbit, partridge, pigeon, and turkey are combined. Seven-meat sancocho is also prepared on special occasions among the people of the Sinú Valley, on the Colombian Caribbean coast, although there the pigeon is replaced by lamb.

42. Buga, for example, was renowned for its jellies. Hamilton wrote that "in Buga they manufacture on a grand scale guava jelly, which reaches numerous remote provinces, for it is considered the best in all of Colombia" (*Viajes por el interior*, 316).

43. Santa Gertrudis, *Maravillas de la naturaleza*, 2:63.

44. This soup owes a good part of its special flavor to the bay leaf in the beef broth in which the beans and corn are cooked and then are added the mixture of leek, parsley, basil, and yerbabuena, with which the cooking is completed. A dollop of sweet cream, at the end, tops it off for serving. Although it has not been said, beans were always customary in the Cauca Valley kitchen, as a side dish on platters or trays, along with meat dressed with yucca and potatoes, slices of ripe plantain, white rice, and salad with avocado. Beans may also serve as a main dish, combined sometimes with green plantain or, at other times, squash.

45. So that it turns out right, the cooking procedure consists of adding the broth bit by bit, as the rice starts to dry.

46. *El carnero* is the scandalous chronicle of the provincial city of Santafé de Bogotá, by Friar Juan Rodríguez Freyle (1566–1642). Originally titled *Crónica de la conquista y descubrimiento del Nuevo Reino de Granada* (Chronicle of the conquest and discovery of the New Kingdom of Granada; written 1636–38 but not published in Colombia until 1859), it is among the first works of narrative written by a Spanish-speaking American.

47. Lovera, *Gastronomía caribeña*, 99

48. Bello, "Repúblicas hispanoamericanas," 179–261.

49. Ibid.

María

1. *María* is a landmark nineteenth-century Colombian novel by Jorge Isaacs, published in 1867 and considered by many critics to stand as an exemplary case of sentimental Romanticism in Latin America. In this essay the novel is employed as a realistic index of patrician agrarian life during the period of the 1830s–60s. Although slavery was abolished in Colombia in 1851, *María* is set prior to that date, thus permitting the author to treat that institution benignly through the narrator's nostalgic eyes.

2. Menton, "Estructura dualística de *María*," 251.

3. Borges, "Vindicación de la *María*."

4. See Romero, *Latinoamérica*.

5. Isaacs, *María*, 8.

6. An "ideophone," a guasá is made with a cylinder of thick bamboo (*guadua*) into which arrowroot seeds are introduced. Isaacs calls them *alfandoques* in the novel.

7. Cited in Witt, *Black Hunger*.

8. This is an excerpt from Aurelio Arturo, in his poem "Nodriza" (Wet nurse), in *Obra e imagen*. There is a good portrait of these proxy mothers in *Gone with the Wind*, by Margaret Mitchell.

9. Jorge Isaacs, "Lo que fue, es, y puede llegar a ser la raza africana en el Cauca," *La República*, July 10, 1867.

10. Sydney Mintz, in his excellent collection of essays, *Tasting Food*, conveys the following quote from Pierre Bordieu, which reinforces the idea: "It is probable that in the flavors of food we find the strongest and most indelible mark of learning in infancy, the lessons that last longest across time, despite the collapse of the world that generated them, and that nostalgia enduringly sustains. The lost universe is, after all, a maternal universe, a world of primordial tastes and basic food, of archetypical relationships and archetypical cultural goodness, in which the pleasure received is an integral part of all pleasures" (10).

11. Freyre, *Masters and the Slaves*, xii; Colmenares, "Cali," 1:117–52.

12. Isaacs, *María*, 58.

13. López Cano, *Tumba de María Isaacs*, 289–90.

14. Xavier Domingo, in *Mesa del buscón*, brings us a reference from the cookbook of Martínez Motiño, *Arte de cocina*, published in the seventeenth century, which describes a dessert made with almond milk and sugar, which after several "hard boilings, is so thick that, upon cooling, may be called dulce de leche" (117). This was the popular version. The noble one, of "power dining," had ground chicken breast, almond milk, and sugar. The dulce de leche of the poor was *despechugado* (deboned breast). Both versions passed over to Latin America, where the almond milk was replaced by cow's milk, to which rice flour was added. José Rafael Lovera, in his *Gastronomía caribeña*, alludes to a Guatemalan recipe book published in 1844 in which dulce de leche is prepared with cow's milk, rice flour, sugar, and chicken breast previously cooked and ground (87). Moreover, the Arab origin of dulce de leche is well documented.

15. Witt, *Black Hunger*.

16. Isaacs, *María*, 5–6. Here we learn that María served the table, an indication of her position of inferiority relative to the rest of the women in the family. A family of the elite like the one portrayed in the novel would have abundant service personnel. That a young lady of the home should occupy herself with this job indicates that she is considered a subordinate. This is a suggestion of the true reason why both of Efraín's parents oppose his marriage to María. It is a matter of a disadvantageous union according to the social canons of the period.

17. Ibid., 37.

18. Cited by González, *Elogio de la berenjena*.

19. Isaacs, *María*, 44, 83.

20. Ibid., 149.

21. Caldas, "Influjo del clima," 75.

22. Domingo, *Mesa del buscón*, 154–55, 154.

23. Ruiz, *Libro de buen amor*, 234–35.

24. Domingo, *Mesa del buscón*, 152

25. Valdivieso et al., *Platos de las abuelas*, 75. That is how the cookbook puts it. Nonetheless, my informants, the black cooks who sell it every year in the marketplace or make it to order, clarify that the process of *desamargar* (unbittering) the rind consumes quite a bit more than three or four days. They speak of ten days at least, changing the water three times per day, suggesting how

necessary this is so that the dessert takes on the flavor it is known for. They also say that the lemons are cooked cut in halves and that the pulp is removed after cooking, not before.

26. Isaacs, *María*, 155.

27. Mintz, *Tasting Food*, 36.

28. Pepita, a young and attractive widow portrayed by Juan Valera in the novel *Pepita Jiménez*, upon becoming a distinguished lady, does not actually cook, but her maid, who does cook, in the guise of a go-between makes a date with her indecisive lover the night of Saint John (June 21), confident of the atmosphere of food and gallantry that impregnates the area. Valera writes, "The evening and morning of St. John, although it is a Catholic feast day, conserves uncertain aftertastes of ancient paganism and naturalism. . . . All was profane, and not religious. All was love and flirtation . . . the many tables of almond paste, fruit syrup, and crispy fried plantains. . . . The kiosks where gypsies young and old were already frying the dough . . . were already weighing and serving the cheese buns" (149). Cuisine and sensuality, sweets and sex, always go together. These days, even in our skeptical cities, Saint Valentine's Day entails a sweet chocolate treat as an obligatory gift between lovers or with suitors.

29. A collection of basic essays on this subject can be found in the book edited by Carole Counihan and Penny van Esternik, titled *Food and Culture*. See there the seminal article: Barthes, "Toward a Psycho-sociology."

30. In this sense it deals with the same idea that Fernand Braudel expresses to explain the cultural unity of Spain and, equally, the governing thought that allows him to perceive the Mediterranean region as a universe that integrates peninsulas, mountains, high plateaus, and plains, beyond the maritime space (*Mediterráneo y el mundo*, 68).

31. Preston, "Crédito y la economía," 17.

32. Mollien, *Viaje por la República*, 300–301.

33. Isaacs, *María*, 5.

34. See Patiño Ossa, "De la navegación."

35. Patiño, *Alimentación y alimentos*, 132.

36. Cieza de León, *Crónica del Perú*, 112–13.

37. According to Santa Gertrudis, from heart of palm comes the best *masato*, a refreshing drink made of lightly fermented fruits or cereals, joined by water and sugar syrup (*Maravillas de la naturaleza*, 86).

38. Isaacs, *María*, 179.

39. Fernández-Armesto, *Historia de la comida*, 37.

40. Arocha, *Ombligados de Ananse*, 99.

41. The book by Valencia, *Sabor del Pacífico*, includes a recipe book based on the testimonies of expert cooks from Bahía Solano, Quibdó, Itsmina, Andagoya, Guapi, Tumaco, and Buenaventura. For the research and fieldwork undergirding it, this is one of the best cookbooks published in all of Colombia.

42. A sauce common to various regions of Latin America, *refrito*, *hogao*, or *sofrito* is obtained by lightly frying in olive oil chopped onions, chunked tomatoes, garlic, and—at times—seedless chili, salt, cumin, and black pepper (when it does not have chili). One can also throw in paprika.

43. Isaacs, *María*, 178.

44. Carvajal, *María*.

45. Revelo Hurtado, *Voces e imágenes*, 88.

46. See "Fufú."

47. See Bartle, "Women III."

48. See Jiménez Soler, "Plátano."

49. Fernández-Armesto, *Historia de la comida*, 255.

50. A *bolinho* is a cooked batter of yucca, potato, plantain, and so on that goes well with meats, fish, vegetables, cheeses, and egg yolks as a binder and then is fried in hot olive oil. Codfish *bolinho* is very popular. A *carimañola* is a cooked yucca dough with meat filling fried in very hot oil. An *aborrajado* is a mashed ripe plantain, breaded and fried and filled with fresh white cheese.

51. Referenced by Mintz, in *Tasting Food*, 44.

52. See Sarasti Aparicio, "Cuando el Cauca era un río."

53. See the reproduction of an engraving by Edouard Riou, in André," fig. 16.

54. Mollien, *Viaje por la República*, 69.

55. Fernández-Armesto, *Historia de la comida*, 121.

56. Isaacs, *María*, 46.

57. Ibid., 47.

58. Ibid., 54.

59. There are exceptions, as occurs with the oyster gatherers in the mangrove swamps of the Colombian Pacific coast, called *piangüeras*, for the name—*piangua*—given to the mollusk the women collect.

60. Mintz, *Tasting Food*, 7.

61. Lévi-Strauss, "Culinary Triangle," 29.

62. Isaacs, *María*, 48–49.

63. Xavier Domingo provides some references from sixteenth-century Spain about *olla podrida*, in which it is indicated that "one must cook bacon (meat that is salted and sun-dried), cow and pig tongues, pig feet and ears, and sausage. Combine all the broths into a vessel, in which you cook vegetables, cabbage, turnip, parsley, camomile, garlic, and onions" (*Mesa del buscón*, 62). The similarity of this traditional Spanish dish to our sancocho is so evident that some of the nineteenth-century European observers continued to call it by the Castilian name, as did Lionel Wafer, when he noted that "the prime base of the Indians' diet consists of maize and plantain. Their preferred food is *olla podrida*, composed of meat—game or domesticated—with as many vegetables as may be procured" (quoted in Patiño, *Alimentación y alimentos*, 243). Patiño wrote that "the basic dish in Peru was *locro*, a soup with dried or fresh llama meat and an abundance of chili, potatoes, or *chuño*—which is dehydrated potato—various legumes, maize, and quinoa" (61).

64. This Dominican friar traveled throughout New Granada in the middle of the eighteenth century. Santa Gertrudis's work, titled *Maravillas de la naturaleza*, focuses especially on dietary habits and allows us to establish how, for the period of his travels, a new Creole culture—a veritable cultural sancocho that integrated the Hispanic, the Afro, and the pre-Hispanic—was predominant at all tables, from the humblest to the most powerful. This helps confirm the fact that the cultural transformations preceded the political and economic transformations, an insight of great importance for Latin American historiography.

65. The same applies to Bogotá's ajiaco, a stew in which potatoes replace the products of the warm country: yucca and plantain. Aída Martínez Carreño provides the following confirmation from Jean Baptiste Boussingault: "The few artisans [of Bogotá] and the peasants sustained themselves especially on ajiaco, which is a mixture of beef or mutton, finely chopped and cooked with potatoes and seasoned with garlic and onions. . . . I contend that it is a very good soup" (*Mesa y cocina*). The Bogotá ajiaco of today, with insipid strings of chicken breast, has little relation to its more robust and tastier forebear. Thanks to the modern addition of heavy cream and capers, it has managed to recover part of its flavor. On the contrary, in the ajiaco of Cuba one still finds shreds of meat, even if at times it may be of chicken, and in Chile—where sancocho is also called ajiaco—the chicken has been replaced by pickled beef, which is first oven roasted and then cut in fine strips and cooked with the remaining components.

66. Isaacs, *María*, 144.

67. Quoted in Patiño, *Relaciones de vísperas*, 530.

68. Ibid. For a very good chronicling of the abundance of edible products in the Cauca Valley countryside, as narrated by the mayors of Cali in 1808, see Patiño, "Relaciones de vísperas."

69. See Frederick Zeuner, *A History of Domesticated Animals*, cited by Patiño, *Alimentación y alimentos*, 186.

70. Colonia and Urdinola, quoted in Patiño, "Relaciones de vísperas," 530; Patiño, *Alimentación y alimentos*, 239.

71. *Biche* is a regionalism for "young" and "unripe." *Biche* fruit is, therefore, green.

72. García, *Escritos escogidos*, 117–47.

73. Evaristo García, who belonged to the elite groups, both intellectual and economic, of the Cauca Valley, establishes a noteworthy distinction in the preparation of sancocho, for the one made in his home did not contain bacon or jerky, while the popular or "cowboy" kind continued to use this cured meat. Perhaps that can be attributed to the fact that, for the period and in a city like Cali, it was already possible to procure fresh meat daily, even though at that time appliances for the refrigeration of food were still unknown in the country. What also stands out is that he foregoes *yerba mate*, an aromatic flavoring leaf that becomes indispensable for achieving the characteristic bouquet of the traditional cuisine of this region of Latin America. At any rate, it is an indication of a social separation regarding taste, which, in the case of García, a physician educated in Paris and London, is easily understood.

74. See Serret, *Viaje a Colombia*.

75. See ibid.

76. The contrast between material poverty and abundance of food is often observed, and it is worth bringing to bear his experience in Cartago, when he reached an inn that was nothing other than an "immense barracks from the era of Don Quixote, all dilapidated and ruined, with the look of a hospital in a poor village," where they served him a magnificent breakfast that "consisted of a fine plate of pumpkin and rice, *tortilla* with tomato, steak *a caballo* [literally 'on horseback'], that is, with a side of fried eggs, one or two slices of pineapple, and an excellent coffee," which he accompanied with a "small glass of rum," to celebrate the robust fare and the fact that it cost so little that he felt it was practically free (Serret, *Viaje a Colombia*, 102–3).

77. Lovera, *Historia de la alimentación*, 99.

78. Appun and Sullivan, quoted in Lovera, *Gastronomía caribeña*, 103.

79. Isaacs, *María*, 148.

80. From another perspective, this participation turns out to be important in the cuisine's modernization. However, in the case at hand, and more generally in the case of Colombia, in cultural matters the elites acted from a prejudiced stance that considered "inferior" anything that might come from Indians, blacks, or mestizos. They suffered from an *arrivisme* toward all things European, which constrained them from playing the role, roughly in the same period, of the French bourgeoisie, which constructed modern cuisine by basing itself on the old regional peasant cuisine (which explains the patés, the *terrines*, the *boillabeuse*, the *pot au feu*, the onion soup, the stuffed sausages, and the hams, etc.) and censured aristocratic cuisine, laden with spices, extravagance, and pretentious exoticisms (pheasant tongues, little birds flying out of the belly of a roast boar, dulce de leche with chicken breast, etc.).

Epilogue

1. Bello, "Repúblicas hispanoamericanas."

BIBLIOGRAPHY

André, Edouard. "L'Amérique équinoxial (Colombie–Equateur–Pérou)" [Equatorial America (Colombia–Ecuador–Peru)]. *Le tour du monde* [Round-the-world tour] 34 (1877): 1–64; 35 (1878): 129–224; 37 (1879): 97–144; 38 (1879): 273–368; 45 (1883): 337–416.

Arocha, Jaime. *Ombligados de Ananse: Hilos ancestrales y modernos en el Pacífico Colombiano* [Initiates of Ananse: Ancestral and modern threads in the Colombian Pacific]. Bogotá: Universidad Nacional de Colombia, 1999.

Arturo, Aurelio. "La nodriza" [The wet nurse]. In *Obra e imagen* [Work and image]. Bogotá: Instituto Colombiano de Cultura, 1997.

Barney Cabrera, Eugenio. *Notas y apostillas al margen de un libro de cocina* [Notes and comments in the margins of a cookbook]. Cali: Universidad del Valle, 2004.

Barthes, Roland. "Toward a Psycho-sociology of Contemporary Food Consumption." In Counihan and Esternik, *Food and Culture*, 20–27.

Bartle, Phil. "Women III: Cooking 1." *Akan Studies*. Last updated November 13, 2014. cec.vcn.bc.ca/rdi/kw-cook.htm.

Bello, Andrés. "Las repúblicas hispanoamericanas: Autonomía cultural" [The Spanish American republics: Cultural autonomy]. In *Antología de discursos y escritos* [Anthology of discourses and writings]. Madrid: Editora Nacional, 1976.

Borges, Jorge Luis. "Vindicación de la *María* de Jorge Isaacs" [Vindication of *María* by Jorge Isaacs]. In *Textos cautivos* [Captive texts]. Buenos Aires: Tusquets Editores, 1986.

Braudel, Fernand. *El Mediterráneo y el mundo mediterráneo en la época de Felipe II* [The Mediterranean and its world in the era of Philip II]. Mexico City: Fondo de Cultura Económica, 1987.

Burgos Cantor, Roberto, ed. *Rutas de libertad: Quinientos años de travesía* [Routes of freedom: Five hundred years of crossing]. Bogotá: Ministerio de Cultura y Pontificia Universidad Javeriana de Colombia, 2010.

Caldas, Francisco José de. "Del influjo del clima sobre los seres organizados" [On the influence of climate on organized beings]. In *Fronteras imaginadas: La construcción de las razas y la geografía en el siglo XIX colombiano* [Imagined frontiers: The construction of race and the geography of nineteenth-century Colombia], edited by Alfonso Múnera. Bogotá: Planeta Editorial, 2004.

Carvajal, Mario, ed. *María*. By Jorge Isaacs. Cali: Biblioteca de la Universidad del Valle, 1967.

Cieza de León, Pedro. *La crónica del Perú* [The chronicle of Peru]. Bogotá: Ediciones Revista Ximénez de Quesada/Editorial Kelly, 1971.

Colmenares, Germán. "Cali: Terratenientes, mineros, y comerciantes" [Cali: Landowners, miners, and merchants]. In *Sociedad y economía en el Valle del Cauca* [Society and economy in the Cauca Valley], 117–52. Vol. 1. Bogotá: Banco Popular, 1983.

Counihan, Carole, and Penny van Esternik. *Food and Culture*. 2nd ed. New York: Routledge, 1997.

Crevaux, J. *Voyages dans l'Amérique du Sud* [Voyages in South America]. Paris: Hachette.

Debret, Jean-Baptiste. *O Brasil de Debret* [Debret's Brazil]. Belo Horizonte: Villa Rica Editoras.

Domingo, Xavier. *La mesa del buscón* [The rogue's table]. Barcelona: Tusquets Editores, 1981.

D'Orbigny, Alcide. *Voyage pittoresque dans les deux Amériques* [Picturesque voyage in the two Americas]. Paris: Tenré, 1993.

Dumas, Alexandre, père. *Grand dictionnaire de cuisine* [Great dictionary of cuisine]. Paris: Lemerre, 1873.

Fernández-Armesto, Felipe. *Historia de la comida* [History of food]. Barcelona: Tusquets Editores, 2004.

Freyre, Gilberto. *The Masters and the Slaves.* Translated by Samuel Putnam. Berkeley: University of California Press, 1986.

"Fufú." *Ikuska.* Accessed March 6, 2020. http://www.ikuska.com/Africa/Gastronomia/Fufu_name.htm.

García, Evaristo. *Escritos escogidos* [Selected writings]. Cali: Feriva, 1994.

González, Abel. *Elogio de la berenjena* [In praise of the eggplant]. Buenos Aires: Vergara Editor, 2000.

Hamilton, Potter John. *Viajes por el interior de las provincias de Colombia* [Travels through the interior of the provinces of Colombia]. Bogotá: Presidencia de la República, 1993.

Holton, Isaac. *La Nueva Granada: Veinte meses en los Andes* [New Granada: Twenty months in the Andes]. Bogotá: Banco de la República, 1981.

Isaacs, Jorge. *María.* Edited by Gustavo Mejía. 1867. Reprint, Caracas: Biblioteca Ayacucho, 1988.

Jiménez Soler, Guillermo. "El plátano, bendición de Fray Tomás" [The plantain, a blessing of Friar Thomas]. *Cuba: Una identità in movimento* [Cuba: An identity in motion]. Accessed April 19, 2020. http://www.archivocubano.org/soler.html.

Kolchin, Peter. *American Slavery.* New York: Hill and Wang, 1993.

Lévi-Strauss, Claude. "The Culinary Triangle." In Counihan and Esternik, *Food and Culture,* 28–35.

López Cano, Luis Francisco. *La tumba de María Isaacs: Genesis y desarrollo de una leyenda vallecaucana* [The tomb of María Isaacs: Genesis and development of a Cauca Valley legend]. Bogotá: Ministerio de Cultura, 2002.

Lovera, José Rafael. *Gastronomía caribeña* [Caribbean gastronomy]. Caracas: Centro de Estudios Gastronómicos, 1991.

———. *Historia de la alimentación en Venezuela* [History of eating in Venezuela]. Caracas: Centro de Estudios Gastronómicos, 1998.

Malinowski, Bronislaw. Prologue to Ortiz, *Contrapunteo cubano,* 4–5.

Martínez Carreño, Aída. *Mesa y cocina en el siglo decimonoveno* [Dining and cooking in the nineteenth century]. Bogotá: Fondo Cultural Cafetero, 1985.

Martínez Motiño, Francisco. *Arte de cocina, pastelería, bizcochería y conservería* [Art of cooking, pastry baking, biscuit baking, and conserve making]. Madrid: Sánchez, 1611.

Menton, Seymour. "La estructura dualística de *María*" [The dualistic structure of *María*]. *Thesaurus* 25 (1970): 251–77.

Mintz, Sydney. *Tasting Food, Tasting Freedom.* Boston: Beacon, 1996.

Mollien, Gaspard. *Viaje por la República de Colombia en 1823* [Voyage through the Republic of Colombia in 1823]. Bogotá: Biblioteca Popular de Cultura Colombiana, 1944.

Ortiz, Fernando. *Contrapunteo cubano del tabaco y el azúcar: Advertencia de sus contrastes agrarios, económicos, históricos y sociales, su etnografía y transculturación* [Cuban counterpoint of tobacco and sugar: Notification of their agricultural, economic, historical, and social contrasts, their ethnography and transculturation]. Madrid: Cátedra, 2002.

Palacios, Eustaquio. *El alférez real* [The royal second lieutenant]. Cali: Silvia Patiño Editora, 2003.

Patiño, Víctor Manuel. *Alimentación y alimentos* [Diet and food]. Vol. 1 of *Historia de la cultura material en la América equinoccial* [History of material culture in equatorial America]. Bogotá: Instituto Caro y Cuervo, 1990.

———. *Del condumio y del yantar* [Of grub and repast]. Vol. 4. Cali: Imprenta Departamental, 1979.

———. "Relaciones de vísperas de la Independencia" [Tales from the eve of independence]. *Revista Cespedesia*, nos. 45–46 (1983).

Patiño Ossa, Germán. "El bienmesabe vallecaucano" [The Cauca Valley's *bienmesabe*]. *El País* (Cali), October 3, 2011.

———. "De la navegación y de la vida ribereña en el Valle colonial" [Of navigation and river life in colonial Cauca Valley]. In Patiño Ossa, *Herr Simmonds*.

———. "El estado natural de la libertad" [The natural state of freedom]. In Burgos Cantor, *Rutas de libertad*.

———. *Herr Simmonds y otras historias del Valle del Cauca* [Herr Simmonds and other stories from the Cauca Valley]. Cali: Comunidad Universitaria Autónoma de Occidente, 1992.

———. "Raíces de africanía en el bambuco" [Roots of Africanness in the Bambuco]. *Pacífico Sur* 2 (2004).

Pérez, Dionisio. *Guía del buen comer español* [Guide to good Spanish eating]. Madrid: Sucesores de Rivadeneyra, 1929.

Preston, Richard H. "El crédito y la economía" [Credit and the economy]. In *Sociedad y economía en el Valle del Cauca* [Society and economy in the Cauca Valley]. Vol. 4. Bogotá: Banco Popular, 1983.

Quevedo y Villegas, Francisco de. *La vida del buscón* [Life of the rogue]. Zaragoza: Verges, 1626.

Revelo Hurtado, Baudilio. *Voces e imágenes del litoral pacífico colombiano* [Voices and images from the Colombian Pacific coast]. Cali: Feriva, 2005.

Rivera y Garrido, Luciano. *Impresiones y recuerdos* [Impressions and memories]. Cali: Carvajal, 1968.

Rodríguez Freyle, Juan. *El carnero: Conquista y descubrimiento del Nuevo Reino de Granada* [The sheepskin: Conquest and discovery of the New Kingdom of Granada]. 1636. Reprint, Caracas: Biblioteca Ayacucho, 1979.

Romero, José Luis. *Latinoamérica: Las ciudades y las ideas* [Latin America: Cities and Ideas]. Medellín: Universidad de Antioquia, 1999.

Romoli, Kathleen. *Colombia: Gateway to South America*. Garden City, NY: Doubleday, Doran, 1941. http://babel.hathitrust.org/cgi/pt?id=mdp.39015017638498.

Ruiz, Juan (Archpriest of Hita). *Libro de buen amor* [Book of good love]. Madrid: Redimat Libros, 1999.

Saffray, Charles. "Voyage à la Nouvelle Grenade" [Voyage to New Granada]. 1869. *Le tour du monde* [Round-the-world tour] 24 (1872): 81–144; 25 (1873): 97–144; 26 (1873): 65–112.

Santa Gertrudis, Friar Juan de. *Maravillas de la naturaleza* [Marvels of nature]. 2 vols. Bogotá: Banco Popular, 1970.

Sarasti Aparicio, Alejandro. "Cuando el Cauca era un río" [When the Cauca was a river]. In *Revista despertar Vallecaucano* [Cauca Valley wake-up call journal]. Cali: Biblioteca Departamental, 1970.

Serret, Félix. *Viaje a Colombia, 1911–1912* [Voyage to Colombia, 1911–1912]. Bogotá: Banco de la República, 1994.

Valdivieso de C., Fanny, et al. *Platos de las abuelas* [Dishes of our grandmothers]. Popayán, 1974.

Valencia, Emilia. *El sabor del Pacífico* [The flavor of the Pacific]. Cali: Dirección de
   Cultura, 2001.
Valencia Llanos, Alonso. *Resistencia militar indígena en la provincia de Popayán*
   [Indigenous military resistance in the province of Popayán]. 2nd ed. Cali:
   Universidad del Valle, 1991.
Valera, Juan. *Pepita Jiménez*. Madrid: M. E. Editores, 1994.
Witt, Doris. *Black Hunger: Food and the Politics of U.S. Identity*. New York: Oxford
   University Press, 1999.

CREDITS

· · · · · · · · · · · · · · · · · · · ·

Photos from Charles Saffray, "Voyage à la Nouvelle-Grenade," and Edouard André, "L'Amérique équinoxiale (Colombie–Equateur–Pérou)," are by Mauricio Osorio.

Fig. 1: Wikimedia Commons (Adrian Pingstone)

Fig. 2: Etching from Charles Saffray, "Voyage à la Nouvelle-Grenade," *Le tour du monde* (*TDM*) 24 (1872). Colección libros raros y manuscritos, Biblioteca Luis Angel Arango, Bogotá

Figs. 3, 6, 12: From Saffray, "Voyage," *TDM* 25 (1873): 140, 105, 136. Colección libros raros y manuscritos, Biblioteca Luis Angel Arango, Bogotá

Figs. 4, 17, 18: Etchings from Edouard André, "L'Amérique équinoxiale (Colombie–Equateur–Pérou)," *TDM* 37 (1879): 127, 123, 103

Figs. 5, 10: From André, "L'Amérique équinoxiale," *TDM* 38 (1879): 299, 311

Fig. 7: From André, "L'Amérique équinoxiale," *TDM* 34 (1877): 38

Fig. 8: From André, "L'Amérique équinoxiale," *TDM* 35 (1878): 200

Figs. 9, 15, 20: Etchings from Alcide D'Orbigny, *Voyage pittoresque dans les deux Amériques* (Paris: Tenré, 1836), after p. 46; before p. 19; after p. 14

Figs. 13, 14: From Saffray, "Voyage," *TDM* 26 (1873): 93, 96. Colección libros raros y manuscritos, Biblioteca Luis Angel Arango, Bogotá

Fig. 16: Watercolor from Debret, *O Brasil de Debret* (Belo Horizonte: Villa Rica Editoras, 1993), 43

Fig. 19: From André, "L'Amérique équinoxiale," *TDM* (1876)

Fig. 21: Etching from J. Crevaux, *Voyages dans l'Amérique du Sud* (Paris: Hachette, 1883), 195

aborrajados—Breaded and fried mashed ripe plantain filled with fresh white cheese.

achiote—A distinctly colored and flavored mainstay of Latin American cooking. Achiote paste is made from the slightly bitter, earthy-flavored, red annatto seeds, mixed with other spices and ground into a paste.

agouti—An aquatic, otter-like, forest-dwelling rodent of darkish color with white markings on its sides, prized for its meat.

aguardiente—Literally "burning water." A popular form of brandy and a major industry of the Cauca River Valley.

ajiaco—Potato soup. Although several regions of Colombia have their distinct recipe, the most famous is that of Bogotá's, the nation's capital, where it is a cultural mainstay. It typically contains pieces of chicken, large chunks of corn on the cob, two or three kinds of native potatoes, and *guasca*, a weedy, aromatic herb common in all America. Ajiaco is so hearty that it is usually considered a full meal. Elsewhere in Latin America, ajiaco can be another name for sancocho.

amito—Young master. A diminutive of *amo* (a term of respect for the authority of the patriarch), *amito* is a term of affection for the young man developing toward that status. See also *patroncito*.

aquil—A scaleless freshwater fish.

arepa—Corn bread, often filled with cheese and/or egg for a satisfying breakfast.

arum—A tuber that may serve as the dough in preparing fufú.

atollado—A creamy textured rice soup.

bala—A kind of dough made from cooked green bananas salted to taste, puréed, and mixed in a base of achiote, with abundant butter and a touch of smashed garlic.

bambuco, bambuco viejo (old *bambuco*)—A popular Caribbean dance of African origin, a strong example of Creole culture.

barbudo—Literally "bearded one." A freshwater fish abundant in the region (*Pimelodus blochi*).

biche—A colloquial term for "green" or "unripe."

bienmesabe—Literally "it tastes good to me." A custard dessert.

bijao—Leaves used to line a cooking pit in preparing a stew, to which food is added before covering it with dirt and lighting a fire.

bocachico—Literally "cute-mouth." An abundant, medium-size freshwater fish, also called gorrón and, in the Chocó region, *chere*.

bolinho—A cooked batter of yucca, potato, plantain, and so on, which goes well with meats, fish, vegetables, cheeses, and egg yolks as a binder, and then is fried in hot olive oil. Codfish *bolinho* is very popular.

boruga—A type of warm *kumis*, drunk before the whey separates from the rest of the milky liquid.

burilico—A conifer (*Xylopia catophylla*) that grows in wetland forests. A valuable source of pine nuts on which pigs feed.

cagüinga—A long wooden spoon, used to beat the dulce de leche.

capybara—Known in Spanish as *chigüiro*, the world's largest rodent (up to thirty pounds), a good source of meat in Cauca Country.

carantanta—A corn-based soup.

carimañola—A cooked yucca dough with meat filling that is fried in very hot oil.

ceviche—A piquant dish long popular along the Pacific seaboard from Colombia to
   Peru, made of fish or shellfish that is cooked not over a stove but by marinating
   it in lemon juice, with onion, garlic, salt, and chili. Its origins are uncertain and
   hotly debated.

champús—A beverage concocted with corn and tropical fruits such as *lulo* or
   guanabana.

chere—Alternate name in Chocó for the freshwater fish bocachico.

chigüiro—See capybara.

chilacoas—Wild foul, alternatively called *chochaperdiz* (*Himantopus mexicanus*), hunted
   in forest clearings.

chontaduro—A product of the *chonta* palm, a sort of panacea plant, providing nutritious
   food, useful leaves, and wood to build shelter and a variety of tools.

chuyaco—Chili-spiced peanuts.

cocada—Grated coconut cooked with brown sugar to form sugary loaves.

coclí—A bird similar to but larger than the heron.

cowboy sancocho—A stew consisting of green plantain, dried salted meat, and cilantro,
   proper to a peasant style of eating and intended to satisfy the hunger of peons,
   travelers, and cattle drivers.

Creole—Term used to describe people or things originating in or proper to the
   Americas, including indigenous and African influences, rather than identifying
   with a Spanish or otherwise European origin.

desamargado—Literally "unbittered." A sweetened citrus compote, also called *letuario*,
   that can be made into crystallized candy.

droits de seigneur—Literally "lord's rights," with specific reference to privileged access to
   the virginity of newlywed servant women.

dulce de leche—A dessert made of milk, sugar, flour, and rice, all ingredients
   grown or raised locally in Cauca Country. It is widely considered a delicacy,
   requires physical strength to whip, and must sit overnight to reach its optimal
   consistency.

empanadas—Pastries, either fried or baked, filled with mixed ingredients, either savory
   or sweet.

escancer—A red wild bean (*Angus fragilis*).

farofa—A Portuguese term for the mixture of tapioca flour, butter, onions, scrambled
   eggs, and salt and pepper, representative of Brazilian cooking.

fufú—Literally "white-white." A dish, made mainly of green banana, pumpkin, or yam
   dough cooked in broth, with numerous variants in form and name throughout
   the Caribbean and tropical regions of Latin America. Also called *marranita, bala,
   mote, jujú, mangú*, or *mofongo*, according to geographic locale.

gamuza—A dessert made of chocolate with corn flour and unrefined sugar.

gorrón—Freshwater fish, prized for high protein and fat content, so abundant among
   certain indigenous tribes that the name was applied by the Spanish to the people
   who caught, ate, and traded the fish. Also called bocachico and, in the region of
   Chocó, *chere*.

guadua—A cylinder of thick bamboo into which arrowroot seeds are introduced to
   make the musical instrument of the *guasá*.

guagua—An aquatic rodent highly appreciated for its delicately flavored flesh. Not to
   be confused with the Caribbean and Canary Island use of *guagua*, which means
   "bus," or in the Chilean sense of "baby." Also called *pacarana* in Spanish.

guama—A very large sweet white bean (*Reynosia guama*).

guasá—A percussion instrument made with a cylinder of thick bamboo (*guadua*) into
   which arrowroot seeds are introduced. The sound produced by shaking the
   cylinder onomatopoetically resembles the name *guasá*.

guatín—A small rodent that lives in the wild (*Dasyprocta cristata*).

hogao—See *refrito.*

iguasa—A small duck (*Chenalopex jubatus*) valued for its tasty meat and abundantly herded.

jetudo—Literally "big-snout." An abundant freshwater fish.

juyungo—In the language of Ecuador's Cayapas, a derogatory term meaning "black man," "monkey," or "devil."

kumis—Also spelled koumiss, coumiss, and so on. An alcoholic beverage traditionally made from fermented mare's milk, which has a higher sucrose content than cow's or goat's milk.

locro—The Quechua word for "stew" in the Inca Empire.

lulo, lulada—Lulo is a tropical fruit (*Solanum quitoense*), similar in shape to the tomato and the basic ingredient of a refreshing popular drink called *lulada.*

malanga—On the Colombian Pacific coast, the name for the Chinese potato, an alternative ingredient in sancocho.

masato de chontaduro—Dessert wine made from the heart of palm.

milpesos—Literally "a thousand pesos." A tree that is a source of oil and whose fruit can be made into a hot drink that is beaten like chocolate.

mulataje—The process of making mulatto, darkening, or Africanizing.

nagüiblancas—Literally "white petticoats." Large white pigeons that, because of their numbers and their ravenous appetite, constituted a threat to crops.

naidí—A palm tree from whose fruit one can make soft drinks, jellies, and preserves and whose bulb serves as the heart of palm.

ñapangas—Mestizas, young women of mixed (Spanish and indigenous) race.

nayo—An abundant freshwater fish found in many of the rivers of Cauca Country.

negritude—A term coined by the Caribbean poet Aimé Césaire to embrace and attempt to capture the spirit of the Afro-descendant people and culture of the world.

negro—Literally "black one." A freshwater fish caught in Cauca Country.

olla podrida—Literally "rotten pot," the word in Castile for "stew." In the Incan Empire the word for a similar phenomenon was *locro.*

paico—Wormwood, a purgative used to get rid of roundworm parasites.

pandebono—Literally "bread of the good kind." A kind of cheese cruller made of corn dough and served golden brown. Also called *almojábana.*

papayuelas—Tree spinach or mountain papayas.

patroncito—Young master (diminutive of *patrón*). See also *amito.*

peje—An abundant fish and dietary staple in Cauca Country.

piangua—A Pacific version of the tamale in which coconut water is used to thin the green plantain dough and whose filling consists of oyster stew in coconut cream and *hogao.*

pintones—Semiripe plantains.

pipián—A type of nonmeat filling for empanadas consisting of red potatoes, toasted and ground peanuts, garlic, tomato, chopped boiled egg, and so on.

pique—A spicy sauce consisting of chopped chili peppers and onions, water, vinegar, cilantro, salt, and sugar, used to accompany a variety of appetizers.

postrera—A dairy beverage taken from cows near weaning.

pusandao—A hearty soup prepared with fish, green plantains, yucca, *refrito,* coconut water, coconut milk, herbs, and salt.

queso fresco—Literally "fresh cheese," a bland, light cheese that is hardly aged at all.

rayado—Literally "striped one." A freshwater fish.

refrito—In Colombia a sauce prepared by frying in olive oil chopped onions, chunked tomatoes, and garlic, with seedless chili, salt, cumin, and black pepper. Not to be confused with Mexican *frijoles refritos* (refried beans).

sabaleta—Literally "small shad." A freshwater fish (*Brycon henni*).

sancocho—Meat-based stew that, with regional variations in name, kind of meat, and accompanying vegetables and spices, is a dietary staple of the masses of the entire region under discussion. It is closely related to regional dishes called ajiaco, *cazuela, olla podrida,* and *puchero.*

sango—A dish proper to the state of Nariño, south of Cauca Country and abutting the Ecuadorian border. It consists of dough made from fried mashed green plantains, to which cracklings are added.

sardinata—A small freshwater fish (*Pellona castelneana*).

sidrayota—Called the "poor man's potato." A cucurbit that grows on a vine and has a large central seed that is, along with the pulp, edible.

stone cheese—An elastic cheese derived from cooking rennet in whey.

sudado—Literally "sweated." A stew or potage cooked in an underground, leaf-lined pit. Also called *viudo.*

tamales—Cauca tamales differ from the Mexican version in that, although they are made with a base of corn, potato, and chili peppers, they are wrapped in a banana leaf and cooked slowly in boiling water.

tapao—Literally "capped." A stew consisting of several layers of fish in sea water, flavored with pieces of plantain, with one layer of fish separated from the others with *bijao* leaves.

tatabro—A mammal resembling a small deer.

tortilla—In nineteenth-century Colombia (as in Spain), an omelet. This sense differs from that of Mexico's, which is a corn-dough pancake used as a wrap for tacos, enchiladas, and so on.

tostadas—An open-faced taco with a crisp base made of mashed green plantains.

veringo—Literally "naked one." A freshwater fish.

viudo—Literally "widower." See *sudado.*

Yanacona—Quechua-derived word meaning "servant."

yerba mate—An aromatic herb and spice, a regional variant of which forms the base of the national beverage of Paraguay, Argentina, and Uruguay.

zambo—In racial mixing, a combination of African and Amerindian blood.